GREAT HISTORIC DISASTERS

THE
DUST BOWL

GREAT HISTORIC DISASTERS

GREAT HISTORIC DISASTERS

THE
DUST BOWL

RONALD A. REIS

CHELSEA HOUSE
PUBLISHERS
An imprint of Infobase Publishing

THE DUST BOWL

Chelsea House
An imprint of Infobase Publishing
132 West 31st Street
New York, NY 10001

Library of Congress Cataloging-in-Publication Data
Reis, Ronald A., 1941-
The Dust Bowl / Ronald A. Reis.
    p.   cm.—(Great historic disasters)
Includes bibliographical references and index.
ISBN 978-0-7910-9737-3 (hardcover : alk. paper)
1. Great Plains—History—20th century. 2. Dust Bowl Era, 1931–1939.
3. Great Plains—Social conditions—20th century. 4. Great Plains—Rural
conditions. 5. Depressions—1929—Great Plains. 6. Droughts—Great
Plains—History—20th century. 7. Dust storms—Great Plains—History—
20th century. I. Title.
F595.R365 2008
978'.032--dc22   2008004952

Chelsea House books are available at special discounts when purchased in bulk quantities for businesses, associations, institutions, or sales promotions. Please call our Special Sales Department in New York at (212) 967-8800 or (800) 322-8755.

You can find Chelsea House on the World Wide Web
at http://www.chelseahouse.com

Text design by Annie O'Donnell
Cover design by Ben Peterson

Printed in the United States of America

Bang KT 10 9 8 7 6 5 4 3 2

This book is printed on acid-free paper.

All links and Web addresses were checked and verified to be correct at the time of publication. Because of the dynamic nature of the Web, some addresses and links may have changed since publication and may no longer be valid.

Contents

Introduction:
Blown in the Wind

I n the 1930s, housewives living on the Great Plains hung wet sheets and blankets over their windows and struggled to seal every crack and gap with gummed paper strips. They fought a daily battle against the wind-howling Dust Bowl in which they lived.

Still, dust filtered in, penetrating wherever air could go. In pots and pans, in baby cribs, in food on the table, dust was everywhere—dust to eat, dust to drink, dust to breathe. Fanning dust left ripples on kitchen floors. By day's end, a scoop shovel was needed to clear a house. Farmers, sitting at their windows, could, in a manner of speaking, count their neighbors' farms "flying by."

Outside, folks tied handkerchiefs or wore surgical masks over their faces and used goggles to cover their eyes. They put Vaseline in their nostrils to block abrasive particles. In some locations, the dust was strong enough to scrape paint off a farmer's buildings. People avoided shaking hands; the static electricity gathered from the storm could knock a greeter flat. People tied themselves to ropes before going to a barn only dozens of yards away. Children's tears turned to mud. Farmers and townsfolk alike feared choking to death on a blast of

7

Bad weather and poor farming techniques resulted in the tragic Dust Bowl of the 1930s. Huge dust storms destroyed crops and property in communities in five U.S. states, fueling the country's economic problems and leaving people hungry and homeless.

dust-filled air. The simplest thing in life, taking a breath, became life-threatening.

Animals wandered lost, literally blinded by the storm. Birds, helpless to escape the onrushing tidal wave of grit, screeched in fright as they desperately sought to outfly advancing dust storms. Horses chewed hay filled with dust particles that sandpapered their gums raw. Sheep choked to death on dust. Dead cattle, when cut open, were found to be filled with pounds of gut-clogging dirt.

On May 9, 1934, a particularly vicious dust storm, similar to the type just described, burst forth from a high-pressure zone over eastern Montana and the Dakotas. Given the prevailing northwest winds out of the Rocky Mountains, the huge wave front blustered eastward, enveloping the vast Great Plains. This one was a duster to remember.

Normally, such an air mass would raise little concern. Crops in the field would pitch and sway with the tempest. Trees would bend and submit to the pressing gales. Folks would seek shelter indoors for the duration, while animals, both wild and domesticated, would simply hunker down.

On this blistering May day, however, as the violent Chinook thrust out of the west, few, if any, crops stood in its path. Prolonged drought had shriveled, killed, or prevented growth of the wheat, barley, and corn plants. In the spring of 1934, much of the treeless Great Plains lay barren and fallow, the soil pulverized and exposed from previous weather torment.

As mighty drafts "harvested" dust from parched fields, the resulting profusion of dirt rose to 15,000 feet, nearly three miles high. Airplane pilots reported having trouble climbing fast enough to escape the onslaught. Eventually, the 900-mile-wide, 1,800-mile-long duster had gathered in its devastating path an estimated 300 million tons of farmland—3 tons for every man, woman, and child alive in the United States. Upon reaching Chicago, 6,000 tons of dirt descended on rooftops, streets, and bewildered nighttime pedestrians.

The rolling air mass spread to the East Coast—and beyond. In New York City, day turned to dusk, as only half the Sun's normal brightness penetrated. Baseball players even had trouble tracking fly balls.

Over Boston, dust fell like snow. Sailors, up to 300 miles out on the Atlantic, stood perplexed as dust, mixed with fog, turned their air a hazy, murky orange. By the time "The greatest dust storm in United States history," according to the *New York Times*, had ended, more than half the nation had been deluged with its "droppings." Many people were convinced that Armageddon was at hand—that Judgment Day had arrived.

This storm brought the plight of Midwest farmers to the attention of eastern urban dwellers. Yet it was not the first

Dust Bowl duster. Nor was a similar storm that arose in South Dakota and reached Albany, New York, on Armistice Day, November 11, 1933. Considered, nonetheless, an omen of the hundreds of windblown miseries to come, the tortured tempest was "a wall of dirt one's eyes could not penetrate, but it could penetrate the eyes and ears and nose," R.D. Lusk reported in the *Saturday Evening Post*. "It could penetrate to the lungs until it coughed up black."

Then, on April 14, 1935, the "mother of all dusters," referred to simply as "Black Sunday," rained its ruin throughout a vast expanse, particularly the high southern Great Plains, centered on the Oklahoma and Texas Panhandles. A man could not see his own hand in front of his face, so black had day turned into night.

Black Sunday, where, according to Timothy Egan in *The Worst Hard Times*, "The storm carried away twice as much dirt as was dug out of the earth to create the Panama Canal," was not the last of the horrors. No blind stroke of nature, the Dust Bowl dusters of the "Dirty Thirties" had their origins in human error: the misuse of a precious resource, the land. What happened, why it happened, how those affected coped, and what can be learned from the tragedy is the story of the Dust Bowl, considered by many to be America's worst prolonged environmental disaster.

1 Where the Buffalo Roam

Two bull bison, each weighing a ton and each about six feet tall and ten feet long, are going head-to-head, their curved horns butting in angry confrontation. It is mating season in mid-nineteenth-century Montana on the upper reaches of the Great Plains, and it is late August.

Moments earlier, each bull had attempted, through a show of bravado, to avoid direct physical contact. Nine-out-of-ten times it would have worked—one bull backing down in the face of huffing-and-puffing dominance. Not now, however.

The younger of the two bulls makes a tactical blunder, exposing his flank to his older, more experienced antagonist. His opponent takes advantage of his position and delivers a fatal blow. In a week or two, the younger bull, weakened, will likely die. The victorious bull, of course, has won "his" cow. In approximately 40 weeks, a calf will be born. The bison herd survives and multiplies.

Bison, also known as American buffalo, have their natural enemies. Wolves will attack calves, at times consuming up to half a small herd's offspring. Grizzly bears can pose a sporadic threat. And bloodsucking ticks use bison as a place to grow. But in this time and place, the bison have few worries. As they travel in massive herds over the vast plains, they reign supreme. Able to withstand temperatures from 20°F below zero to 120°F above, the awesome creatures dominate and grow. And though with their shaggy brown coats, and massive heads and forequarters, buffalo look cumbersome and slow to move, they can jump up to 6 feet high and run up to 40 miles per hour. They are not to be trifled with. Bison are the Great Plains's keystone breed. Shortly before the Civil

Hunting Buffalo— A Matter of Survival

Hunting buffalo may have been sport for the white man, but it was a matter of survival for Native Americans. For the Plains Indian hunters, the buffalo was the largest source of food, decorations, and crafting tools. Hide, hair, tail, hoof and feet, horns, meat, skin of hindleg, rawhide—not a single part of the animal was wasted.

Riding horses, Native Americans could overtake a buffalo, shooting the beasts at point-blank range with a specially designed, reduced-size bow. Even with the introduction of rifles, most Plains Indians preferred to stick to bows and arrows, finding guns too heavy and difficult to load on a moving horse.

Only the bravest men were allowed to hunt buffalo. They followed strict rules, keeping quiet and advancing only in groups. It was not an easy task to kill a buffalo, but, to sustain a tribe, it had to be done.

War, they were the most numerous single species of large, wild animal on Earth.

Just how expansive these beasts became in their heyday is open to some debate. One authority, the late Dale Lott (author of *American Bison*), put the number at nearly 30 million, though less-informed investigators are often willing to double that figure. Even when split into numerous herds, a sea of brown prevailed. An earlier traveler could spend days moving cautiously among the plodding mammals. Some herds stretched for mile upon mile over the flat, near-empty Great Plains.

To survive and multiply, such an animal needed to minimize contact with predators, and also to find plenty to consume in its typical 18- to 20-year life span. The Great Plains provided buffalo with abundance. The buffalo ate buffalo grass, or prairie sod—"God's grass, the native carpet of plenty," as author Timothy Egan called it.

THE LONE PRAIRIE

Early maps of the Great Plains referred to it as "The Great American Desert." Late-seventeenth- and early eighteenth-century explorers were little impressed with the land that stretched from southern Canada on the north to northern Mexico on the south, with the Rocky Mountains to the west and the Mississippi River on the east. All they saw of the little ground they actually traversed was a featureless flatland—except for an unending mass of grass.

Today, the Great Plains is known as "America's Breadbasket"—a cornucopia of wheat, barley, and corn. It was not always so. Up until recently, the Great Plains was thought good for only one thing—feeding buffalo. The one-million-plus square miles of Great Plains began forming about 20 million years ago. As the uplifted Rocky Mountains in the west drained their snowpacks, deposits of rock and debris flowed eastward. Eventually, over millions of years, the huge basin that is the Great Plains was filled in. Glacier rubble, too, contributed to the earth mass, as periodic waves of ice fields, in some cases two miles thick, expanded and contracted.

With the Rocky Mountains acting as a "rain shadow" partially blocking moist air from the Pacific, the western part of the prairie dried out to become semi-arid. Today, the region is, in some locations, a virtual desert.

Then there is the wind, continuous and intense, with its ever-present gusts and gales. Winter, spring, summer, or fall, the winds are there. In the winter, freezing "northers," as they are called, can put ice on parts of Texas and Oklahoma. During summer, warm air from the Gulf of Mexico and hot, dry air from the Southwest can turn parts of the Great Plains into an outdoor oven.

Thus the climate and weather patterns of the Great Plains contributed to a soil-rich land that, above all else, favored grasses. In the easternmost third of the plains, where rains are more plentiful (up to 40 inches a year), tallgrasses, such as Indian grass and switchgrass, are found. Big bluestem grass can grow 12 feet high and at a rate of half an inch a day. (Mothers would worry that their playful children would get hopelessly lost in its fibers, trapped as in a maze.)

West of the tallgrass belt are the mixed grasses. Rainfall here is diminished, from 23 to 30 inches a year, and the soil is less productive than farther east. Mixed grasses, such as little bluestem, green needlegrass, and prairie dropseed, grow waist-high.

The shortgrass plains, westward, in the reflection (rain shadow) of the Rockies, has an annual rainfall of less than 15 inches. Plants grow 6 to 12 inches high. Buffalo grass dominates the region. It is, for the most part, where the millions of bison, before their near extermination by humans, chose to roam.

AMERICA'S SERENGETI

Even as humans arrived and eventually spread on to the Great Plains by way of the "Bering Land Bridge," the bison continued to multiply. Indians, dressed to deceive in buffalo skins, successfully scared small herds into snowdrifts and onto ice sheets, and then killed them with bladed spears. But such hunting methods, developed over the centuries, hardly made a dent in bison numbers. The bison had been living on the land for at least 5,000 years.

Things changed significantly for Native People, however, when Spaniards reintroduced horses in the late-sixteenth century. By 1700, Plains Indians were racing horses alongside stampeding buffalo, thrusting lances into their bellies or launching arrows from their sinew-strung bows. The kill count went up considerably. But still the buffalo herds grew.

When the Civil War ended in 1865, however, the hunt for buffalo took on a new, deadlier twist. The white man had found sport in killing bison. Aided by the development of a new, powerful killing tool, the Sharps Sporting Rifle, hunters descended on the Great Plains for the fun of the kill. This weapon provided a breech mechanism strong enough to handle the large cartridges needed to kill buffalo at great range. The vast American prairie quickly became the "new" Serengeti; it was *the* place to hunt large, wild animals.

Perhaps the most famous of such buffalo hunters was Buffalo Bill Cody. In January 1872, he took Grand Duke Alexis of Russia on a safari rivaling anything East Africa had ever seen. Preparation for the hunt included six ambulances, 20 extra saddle horses, and a company of cavalry soldiers led by none other than General George Armstrong Custer. In just one day, the hunt yielded 56 bison trophies.

Still, even with the killing of American buffalo as sport, buffalo continued to roam, continued to find pasture, and, if not to increase, to at least sustain themselves.

It was the post–Civil War government policy of moving Plains Indians off the plains and onto reservations in order to promote cattle ranching that first took a serious toll on buffalo numbers. The reasoning was simple: If you killed the buffalo, you destroyed the Indians' source of sustenance.

In an attempt to displace Native Americans, the new Americans settling in the Great Plains aggressively hunted buffalo, the Indians' primary food source. Buffalo Bill Cody *(above left)* worked with the U.S. government to establish hunting seasons as a means to protect the animals from extinction, as well as advocating for the fair treatment of Native Americans.

General Philip Sheridan, of the United States Army, summarized the "unofficial" government view on extermination, both animal and man, when he told the Texas legislature in 1875: "These men (the buffalo hunters) have done more in two years, and will do more in the next two years, to settle the vexed Indian question, than the entire regular army has done in thirty years.... Let them kill, skin, and sell until the buffaloes are exterminated.... Then your prairie can be covered with speckled cattle and the festive cowboy. . . forerunner of an advanced civilization."

That said, there is no question about what finally brought the American buffalo to near extinction in a matter of a decade—the discovery, in the early 1870s, of a method of tanning buffalo hides. Commercial hunting for buffalo skins, now used for everything from luggage to industrial conveyer belts, was the final, devastating development that did the bison in.

The herds could not withstand the big, commercial enterprises organized to take them out. According to *The American People: Creating a Nation and a Society, Volume II*, "Teams of one or two professional hunters, backed by a team of skinners, gun cleaners, cartridge reloaders, cooks, wranglers, blacksmiths, security guards, teamsters, and numerous horses and wagons, took to the plains. Men were even employed to recover and re-cast lead bullets taken from the carcasses."

In a single two-year period, 1872–1873, government agents estimated that nearly 25 million buffalo were killed. By decade's end, the job was done. The country was lucky if in the mid-1880s there were a thousand wild buffalo left on the Great Plains.

AMERICAN COWBOY

With the buffalo gone, and the Indians killed or driven onto reservations in places such as the Oklahoma Territory, the Great Plains's ecology was torn asunder. Buffalo and sod had existed in a symbiotic relationship for thousands of years. Now that one element, the buffalo, had been removed, there needed to be a replacement. Cattle seemed to be a good substitute. The demand for beef was there. With cities expanding in the East, the market for cattle products, food and otherwise, exploded. Getting steers to their destination was the problem, however.

In some cases, herds had to be driven up to 1,200 miles to railheads, such as the one in Kansas City, Missouri. There, cattle were loaded onto railroad stock cars and transported live ("on-the-hoof") to regional processing centers. Cattle that were not then slaughtered for local markets were smoked and shipped east in barrels of salt. The cattle drive was a wasteful, draining process, with cattle losing precious pounds along the way or dying prematurely. With the invention of refrigerated railcars in the early 1870s, however, cattle could be dressed, or prepared, locally and sent east under cold storage. If done correctly, cattle ranching on the Great Plains in the last quarter of the nineteenth century could be quite profitable.

Enter the American cowboy, or, more to the point, the Texas cattleman.

In 1879, the Texas legislature, wanting to build the biggest state capital in the nation, appropriated 3 million acres of land to finance its construction. A Capitol Syndicate of investors was formed that would construct the capital for around $3 million in exchange for the agreed-upon acreage in the western part of the Texas Panhandle.

Known as the XIT Ranch, because the initials formed a brand that was hard to alter and thus would thwart rustlers, the vast spread would, in time, become the largest ranch under fence in the world. By 1887, the XIT employed 150 cowboys, riding 1,000 horses and branding 35,000 calves a year. Cowboys lived at various stations on the ranch but went into the local towns, extensions of rail feeder lines, to whoop it up on weekends. It was the Wild West of the twentieth-century American imagination.

But the XIT had trouble making money. In fact, it never had a profitable year. Cattle, unlike buffalo, are fragile creatures. In particular, they do not like cold weather. The winter of 1885–1886 nearly wiped out cattle herds throughout the southern plains. The following season, the same thing happened up north. According to Timothy Egan, "Cowboys joked that they could walk the drift line, where snow piled up along fences north of the Canadian River, for 400 hundred miles, into New Mexico, and never step off a dead animal."

XIT investors became nervous. Maybe it was time to put their original game plan into action, one that envisioned selling off the ranch in parcels for agriculture use. To do that, of course, they would need to promote settlement. The public would need to be convinced that the miles and miles of prairie sod, which had never been turned over to any extent, could be farmed. Sodbusters would have to be lured into the southern Great Plains.

DROUGHT, WIND, AND FIRE

Droughts, blizzards, hailstorms, flash floods, tornadoes, grass fires—living on the Great Plains, particularly the high, southern plains, meant exposure to such varied weather moods (and natural disasters), which were rarely found elsewhere on Earth. Add unrelenting winds, with few if any natural barriers to inhibit their flow, and it was a tough place to make a go of it. When wind and drought combined with lack of vegetation, the latter resulting from prairie fires, there existed a phenomenon that, while not unique to the Great Plains, was, nonetheless, a dominant naturally occurring characteristic—the dust storm.

In 1855, the (Lawrence) *Kansas Free State* newspaper reported: "The dust, which is most annoying, is a resultant of the burning of the prairies, and will not exist after the annual fires have abated. Neither will they harm us after the grass shall get high enough to prevent the wind from taking up the surface, and hurling it with so much force through the atmosphere."

In the spring of 1893, a Nebraska farmer recalled, as reported in Douglas Hurt's *The Dust Bowl*, "Every time we went out of doors in this storm, it was necessary to wear rags of some kind over our faces to keep the sand from literally cutting the skin off our bodies."

Drought, wind, and fire were what made the "dusters." However, in spite of droughts (some lasting years), the unplowed grasslands of the Great Plains were not subject to

After buffalo were hunted to near extinction, cattle were brought in to supply the rising demand for beef in the growing cities of the eastern United States. Cattle ranches like Texas's XIT *(above)* proved a tremendous drain on natural land resources.

major soil erosion. The deep, interconnecting roots of prairie sod grasped the soil. And the roots reached down for the little water there was.

XIT cowboys had to dig down for water, too. The cattle, unlike the buffalo they replaced, needed more to drink than what the heavens could provide. Throughout the huge ranch expanse, no less than 325 water-pumping windmills were required to suck liquid from the huge Ogallala Aquifer, one of the world's largest underground lakes. For cattle to survive on the Great Plains, human intervention was required.

To grow crops, however, would require pure luck. Late-nineteenth- and early twentieth-century technology did not allow for bringing an aquifer's water up in significant quantities for irrigation purposes. For farmers to succeed on the southern plains, they would have to look skyward for water. It was a chancy proposition, something XIT cowboys knew only too well. As their way of life retreated and the cowhands saw sodbusters moving in, they had a warning for their new neighbors: "The Panhandle is no place to break sod! The Panhandle is good for only one thing—growing grass."

2 Wheat Fields Rising

"**N**o Man's Land" they called it—a strip of flat prairie, 35 miles wide and 210 miles long, lying between the Texas Panhandle on the south and Kansas on the north. The name was a legal description, since the land was not attached to any state or territory until 1890. "Miles to water, miles to wood, and only six inches to hell," XIT ranch hands described it, as reported in *The Worst Hard Time*. It was the most wind-raked, least arable part of the Great Plains. "No Man's Land" became the epicenter of the Dust Bowl dusters to come.

The Homestead Act of 1862 brought settlers west at the close of the Civil War, slowly at first, then in a virtual stampede. Passed by Congress to stimulate settlement of the plains, the act offered each head of a household a quarter section (160 acres) and free ownership after five years. The appeal was irresistible to those seeking the Jeffersonian dream, where every man is a rural landowner. Homesteaders would eventually turn over 400 million acres of prairie sod into farmland.

If folks did not come to the plains of their own volition, they would be drawn there by those eager to sell them what free homesteading failed to provide. Railroads required settlers,

Eager to settle Americans into the Plains area, the U.S. government passed the Homestead Act of 1862, providing land and ensuring ownership to would-be farmers who were unfamiliar with the area's land and climate. Encouraged by the bumper crops, people moved west to find their fortunes in farming.

customers, and freight to make a profit. Towns needed growth and development. And land speculators demanded profits. All combined to lure poor, land-hungry dirt farmers into what they were promised would be a Garden of Eden in the "last-chance" West.

There was that problem of water, however, or the lack thereof. But promoters assured the skeptical that plowing, planting, and tending the crops would bring on the water. And sure enough, during the first large-scale agricultural settlement of the Great Plains, particularly the southern plains, during the last decades of the nineteenth century, the rains did come. From 1880 to 1900 (a short, severe, late-1880s drought not withstanding), precipitation was above average, and the first crops flourished. Settlers were encouraged. More and more of them trekked west.

Indeed, the common wisdom of the time claimed that as such "nesters" settled in, the better the climate would actually become. The Timber Culture Act of 1873 was based on the bizarre belief that if folks planted trees, doing so would encourage rainfall. It would not be the last time promoters would claim that "rain followed the plow."

Yet turning a profit, taking the land beyond subsistence, would prove difficult. "I tell you Auntie no one can depend on farming for a living in this country," a Kansas home-steader wrote in a letter, as reported in *The American People*. "We have sold our small grain. . . and it come to $100; now deduct $27.00 for cutting, $16.00 for threshing, $19.00 for hired help. . . and where is your profit? . . . If one wants trials, let them come to Kansas."

Still, in spite of it all, that is what they did. "No Man's Land" witnessed the greatest land boom in its history. By the time Oklahoma became a state in 1907, 32,000 settlers had moved into the Panhandle. By 1910, farmers claimed almost the entire southern plains, with wheat the cash crop of choice.

LIVING WHERE THE LIVING AIN'T EASY

"So here I am, away out in that narrow strip of Oklahoma between Kansas and the Panhandle of Texas, 'holding down' one of the prettiest claims in the Beaver County strip," began homesteader Caroline Henderson in a letter to a friend, repub-lished in *Letters from the Dustbowl*. "I wish you could see this wide, free western country, with its great stretches of almost level prairie, covered with the thick, short buffalo grass, the marvelous glory of its sunrises and sunsets, the brilliancy of its starlit sky at night."

Such optimism and hope often turned to anxiety and despair, however, when prairie farmers began to understand what few resources were at their disposal. Everything, it would seem, had to be brought in, so little did nature provide. And if one did not live within a half-day's buggy ride of a train depot, the only recourse was to look downward, to make do with what was at your feet.

At no time was this more apparent than when it came to building a house, a dwelling to provide protection against the cruel world of blizzards, hailstorms, snow, rain, blistering heat, and the perennial winds.

With no forests on the plains, there was no wood for construction. In frustration and resignation, poor farmers turned to the only asset available in abundance. In order to make bricks, they broke up the very earth they were there to farm. Such farmers constructed their homes from sod, dirt, and grass.

Tearing sod out of the ground in the last half of the nineteenth century was not an easy task. Sod, the top layer of earth, includes grass, its roots, and the dirt clinging to the roots. Tough and tenacious, having evolved to hang on, the roots gripped the soil and held moisture. Jokingly called "Nebraska marble," it took more than a hoe and rake to take sod up.

What was required, of course, was a plow. But not just any plow. The prairie farmer, it soon became apparent, needed a "singing plow," a type developed by John Deere in 1837. Given its nickname because of the whine the plow made as it cut through roots and earth, the steel-tipped moldboard did the job.

House construction began with the cutting of sod bricks 18 inches wide and 24 inches long. Each brick weighed around 50 pounds. It took approximately 3,000 bricks to build a 16 X 20-foot dwelling. Bricks were laid root-side up so the roots would continue to grow into the brick above it. Over time, the bricks grew together to form a strong, tightly bound wall.

Without the typical resources ordinarily used to build houses, like concrete, lumber, and stone, settlers were forced to dig up the midwestern sod to construct their homes. The Chrisman sisters, seen here in 1886 in front of their sod house, held three homestead claims among them and used the land to establish their family in Nebraska state history.

It took time, lots of it, to build such a house because homesteaders soon realized that they should not cut more bricks than they could use in a day. If not stacked soon after cutting, sod quickly dried, cracked, and crumbled.

The roof was the most difficult and chancy home-construction phase. Layers of brush tied into bundles, along with mud and sod, were supported by a series of cedar poles. Such roofs were a constant source of concern and irritation. According to the *National Museum of American History*, "Dirt or water, depending on the weather, fell from the ceiling most of the time. People hung muslin sheets from the ceiling to keep dirt from dropping into their food or an occasional snake from falling on to their beds. Roofs that became too wet sometimes collapsed."

And, yet, still the farmers came, determined to succeed, even though 50 percent of all homesteaders would eventually fail.

PLOW, PLANT, AND HARVEST

Success, however, did not mean merely surviving, subsisting on what varied garden crops could be coaxed out of the ground and what a few farm animals might provide. The prairie farmers had come to make a living from the land. They sought to raise crops to sell, to earn money. Farmers wanted to be businessmen and to be commercial farmers who sold a commodity to local and distant markets. For the vast majority of them, from the 1880s on, that product would be wheat.

Cultivation of wheat as a food grain goes back a long way, 9,000 years, to the Middle East. But it was Russian immigrants, settling in Kansas in the mid-nineteenth century, who got wheat growing in America. They brought with them Turkey red wheat, a hardy variety that is planted in the fall and harvested in the spring. In good times, when the rains came, the Great Plains loved and nurtured it.

While wheat straw will provide livestock bedding, and the green forage is there for grazing, it is the wheat kernel that is turned into food for humans. There are approximately 50 kernels in a head of wheat. Each kernel, in turn, consists of bran, endosperm, and germ. When the kernel is ground into flour, the flour can be used to make bread.

Taking wheat from seed kernel to breakfast toast involves many steps and processes. The farmer's job is to plow the land, plant the seed, and harvest the wheat. A man marching on foot behind a horse was lucky if an acre got plowed in a day. With the introduction of the riding plow, in the late 1870s, however, the acreage plowed leaped sevenfold.

Then, on large farms in the last two decades of the nineteenth century, the horse glimpsed his eventual replacement when steam-powered "road locomotives," or tractors, appeared. Bulky and too expensive for all but the wealthiest farmers, the "traction steam engine," as it was referred to at the time, could easily plow 45 acres in a day. When the steam monsters began to be replaced by gas-powered "automobile plows" in the second decade of the twentieth century, the acreage farmed increased even more.

With new, improved farm implements such as tractors, reapers, threshers, and combines (harvesting machines that clean grain while moving across a field) coming on the market one after the other, as the nineteenth turned into the

The Invention of Barbed Wire

"Don't fence me in," is a common phrase identified with the free-roaming, free-spirited cowboy of the late nineteenth century. But the truth is, fences were needed throughout the Great Plains to keep cattle in their place and away from cultivated farmland. Yet with little wood to construct extensive barriers, somebody had to come up with a fencing that would work, while leaving the few precious trees there were for posts. Joseph F. Glidden, of Dekalb, Illinois, was the man who did it—the man who invented barbed wire.

Eventually, what Glidden patented in 1874 morphed into more than 570 versions of a wire fashioned with barbs at fixed intervals. When livestock first encountered the new barrier, it was usually a painful experience. Some religious groups took to calling it "The Devil's Rope."

twentieth century, a Great Plains farmer discovered he could make a decent living. That is, as long as moisture-laden clouds watered his fields.

BOOM OR BUST ON THE SOUTHERN PLAINS

Clouds, their presence forever questionable, did not always deliver. In fact, in the 20-year period from 1895 to 1915, major droughts occurred throughout the 5-state southern plains—from Nebraska south into Texas, and west to east from Colorado to Arkansas.

In 1885, the dry fall and winter killed much of the Oklahoma wheat crop. When farmers began to plow the crop under, fierce winds blew much of the pulverized soil away. And on March 28, 1896, the first major dust storm of the season struck Dickinson County, Kansas. Drought was followed by wind-carrying plowed-up dirt—a bad omen.

In the first few years of the twentieth century, more droughts, followed by more dust storms, spread throughout the southern plains. From 1910 to 1914, Kansas was as dry as it would be in the 1930s, when dusters created the Dust Bowl. In the spring of 1912, farmers in Thomas County, Kansas, reported that a 15-mile-long and 5-mile-wide strip of land simply blew out. Robert Hurt, writing in *The Dust Bowl*, declared, "Not a sprig of vegetation remained to hold the soil, and the ground was as hard as a city street. . . . The dust storm which this blowout created lasted only several hours, but it was severe enough to make travel hazardous and it forced residents to light lamps."

Drought and then dust storms; it was becoming a pattern. Land left exposed by farmers plowing up every bit of sod they could was creating real problems. It was causing topsoil to fly away.

Yet still they came.

There was money to be made in growing wheat. And the more land a farmer plowed, the more he could earn, given the economics of scale provided by new, powered farm machinery. If one bought a tractor, a huge expense, it needed to be used. Land must be cultivated, torn up.

Many farms, however, remained too small to be economically viable. Even a half-section (320 acres) was often not enough. As a result, some farmers gave up and left; they went back to where they came from. "In God we trusted, in Kansas we busted," the saying went. Nonetheless, the reverse flow of the Great Plains boom-bust cycle never approached the incoming waves of settlers. Drought or not, optimism prevailed.

"Last year was rather disappointing to us in some ways," Caroline Henderson wrote to a friend on January 20, 1912. "Our farm often reminds me of a man who when asked to embark upon some rather doubtful business venture replied that if he wanted to gamble he would prefer roulette, I believe, where the chances were only 32 to 1 against him…. But we are hoping that the years to come may prove that our faith in the future of our big lonely country was not mistaken."

BLOCKADE AT THE DARDANELLES

In 1914, halfway around the world, in a place most Midwesterners, in fact most Americans, could not find on a map, there occurred an event that would serve American wheat farmers well. It would restore, in a perverted way, their faith in farming the Great Plains. The Turks blockaded the Dardanelles.

A narrow strait in northwestern Turkey, separating Europe and the Asian mainland, the Dardanelles—a name derived from Dardania, an ancient Greek city—is 38 miles long and only three-quarters of a mile wide at its narrowest point. The strait empties into the Aegean Sea on the south, which in turn spills into the vast Mediterranean. On the north, the Dardanelles flows into the Sea of Marmara and on through the Bosporus, into the larger Black Sea. The Mediterranean Sea provides agricultural product distribution for most of southern Europe. The Black Sea is an embarkation point for ships car-

Many people saw the Homestead Act as their ticket to prosperity, home ownership, and a future for their family. *Above*, homesteaders gather in Oklahoma in 1901 to make land claims. Under homestead laws, farmers and other settlers could file a claim on designated public land, live on it, and cultivate the land to make it their own.

rying goods from parts of Russia. Prior to 1914, one such commodity was Russian wheat, grown on the vast western steppes.

With the outbreak of World War I in late 1914, the Turks, one of the Central Powers in the conflict, sought to block Allied ships, particularly those of Britain and France, from entering the Dardanelles at its southern point. They blockaded the narrow passageway with more than 350 mines. The blockade was successful in keeping the Allied Powers at bay, and it also kept Russian wheat from entering the Mediterranean Sea. With no Russian wheat to feed the millions of soldiers fighting in the heart of Europe, the desperate Western Allies turned to farmers in the Midwestern United States. As a result, American wheat prices rose significantly, and they stayed up throughout the war, from 1914 to 1918.

In 1910, the price of wheat in the United States stood at 80 cents a bushel. Five years later, thanks to the war, it had doubled. All of a sudden, farming the Great Plains, dry spells aside, looked profitable. According to Timothy Egan, "In less than ten years, [farmers] went from subsistence living to small business-class wealth, from working a few hard acres with horses and hand tools to being masters of wheat estates, direct-ing harvests with wondrous new machines, at a profit margin in some cases that was ten times the cost of production."

With Russian shipments blocked, when the United States entered the war in 1917, the government issued a proclama-tion to the farmers: "Plant more wheat; wheat will win the war!" Furthermore, the government was willing to guarantee grain prices, at two dollars a bushel, throughout the conflict. "Wheat," as Egan pointed out, "was no longer a staple of a small family farmer but a commodity with a price guarantee and a global market."

The farmers, to be sure, promptly grew more wheat. By 1917, about 45 million acres of wheat were harvested through-out the country, most of it from the Great Plains. By 1919, at the close of the war, that number had shot up to 75 million acres, an increase of 70 percent in just two short years.

Could it last? Could farmers continue to tear up marginal lands, those never intended to grow anything but wild grass? Could dry farming on lands with little rain remain viable? And what of the effects of the war, the war that was now over. What would happen to wheat prices as a new decade dawned? What would the 1920s bring to the self-anointed "wheat kings" of the Great Plains?

3 The Good Times and the Bad

World War I had devastated and destroyed. Europe was crippled and exhausted. More than 65 million men had been mobilized, of which more than 10 million died and 20 million were wounded. Of those numbers, approximately 4.7 million Americans served, with 53,402 dying in battle and another 63,114 succumbing to various diseases and related causes. No less than 204,002 Americans were injured.

As American doughboys (infantrymen) returned home in the spring of 1919, citizens greeted them with enthusiasm and lavish victory parades. As Frederick Lewis Allen reported in *Only Yesterday*: "Not yet disillusioned, the nation welcomes its heroes—and the heroes only wished the fuss were all over and they could get into civilian clothes and sleep late in the mornings and do what they please, and try to forget."

But with World War I over, a new trauma was just beginning. Soldiers, fresh from the trenches of Europe, brought back with them something that had actually originated at home, in the heart of the Great Plains. On March 11, 1918, a young army private named Albert Mitchell had reported to the army hospital at Fort Riley, Kansas, complaining of fever, sore throat, and a headache. By noon, more than a 100 soldiers had come down with the same symptoms. In a week, 500 were sick. Forty-eight would eventually die. The recruits had the flu—a killer flu.

Thus began the devastating worldwide influenza pandemic of 1918–1919. The death toll would eventually reach 50 million. In the United States, an estimated 675,000 perished, almost six times the dead the country had suffered in the Great War. As a new decade dawned, America was still recovering from war and disease. It desperately wanted normalcy; it wanted to live and let live in the decade to come.

In all manner of invention, style, and pleasure, Americans now embraced the "Roaring Twenties" with gusto. By 1921, radio broadcasts were a reality. That same year, the World Series broke records for gate receipts and attendance. Babe Ruth hit 59 home runs. In the summer of 1921, Atlantic City held its first beauty pageant. "For the time being, the censor ban on bare knees and skin-tight bathing suits was suspended," wrote a bug-eyed reporter, as noted by Allen. "Thousands of spectators gasped as they applauded the girls." Indeed, women's skirts were rising ever higher and revealing ever more as the 1920s charged on. The hemline was soon to reach an alarming nine inches above the ground. "Flappers wore thin dresses, short-sleeved and occasionally (in the evening) sleeveless," the *New York Times* reported. "Some of the wilder young things rolled their stockings below the knees, revealing to the shocked eyes of virtue a fleeting glance of shin-bones and knee-cap."

On the dance floor, with couples moving ever closer to each other, the *Catholic Telegraph* of Cincinnati reported, "No longer did even an inch of space separate them; they danced as if glued together, body to body, cheek to cheek."

As the 1920s pressed forward, Americans began to enjoy a standard of living unimagined at the dawn of the century. With family income averaging $1,500 per year nationwide, the tide of prosperity was in full flood. Or so it would seem. Farm income throughout the decade averaged a mere $790 per year, only half the national average.

THE GREAT PLOW UP

As expected, wheat prices took a dive after the war. Having reached a peak of $2.75 a bushel in 1918, a farmer was now lucky to get a buck a bushel. With the war over, soldiers having returned to civilian life, and the Dardanelles opened to shipping once more, American farmers were in for a rough decade.

Great Plains farmers were soon confronted with two choices: They could cut back, reduce their acreage in wheat and other staples, and by doing so decrease supply, increase demand, and thus hope prices would rise. Or they could simply plant even more acreage, break more sod, to offset economic loss. They chose the latter.

As wheat acreage increased, farm size also grew. From 1925 to 1930, an average farm went from 780 acres to 812 acres. Much of that additional surface, however, was in submarginal land, with the increasing likelihood of crop failures and vulnerability to drought.

Still, large-scale farming seemed a good bet, at least as long as the rains came. And, for most of the decade, they did.

So enticing was the prospect of "hitting a crop"—making a killing by growing wheat—that the plains now attracted a new kind of farmer, though in most cases he never drove a tractor or harvested a kernel of wheat. Known as "suitcase" farmers or city speculators, these men might not even show up at the farm. They bought farms and let others do the "dirt" work.

"Since wheat planting and harvesting takes only about six weeks a year, individuals living several hundred miles from their fields could engage in wheat farming provided they had the necessary access and equipment to do the work quickly," Douglas Hurt observed. "Many suitcase farmers had their own tractors, and automobiles provided convenient transportation to their lands."

For a time, wheat farming proved to be a lucrative business. The overproduction of that crop and the end to World War I resulted in a supply that was greater than demand. It also led to destruction of the land and favorable conditions for dust storms.

In 1921, a suitcase farmer in Greeley County, Kansas, broke 32,000 acres. Three years later, he was up to 50,000 acres.

Such speculators, with no tie to the land, thought nothing of pulling out if economic conditions warranted. Often in doing so, they simply let the land go fallow, or unplanted during growing season. Drought and dust soon followed.

All told, in the southern plains from 1925 to 1931, wheat acreage expanded 200 percent. Throughout the Great Plains, 32 million acres of sod had been torn up. Overproduction was the inevitable result. Wheat prices fell. And farmers, needing to borrow to stay afloat (to pay for all that additional acreage and the equipment to service it), descended ever deeper into debt.

TRACTORED OUT

When, during the war, the government guaranteed wheat prices at an unheard of two dollars a bushel, farmers, with small and large farms alike, reaped the benefits. However, as soon as the war ended, any good times "real" farmers had experienced became a thing of the past. In 1920, wheat prices fell, on average, to 67 cents a bushel. And yet the land continued to be farmed, plowed under to grow ever more wheat. How much grain did the country, the world, need? Less, much less, it turned out, than was being dumped onto the market.

It soon got to the point where small farmers, with their debts piling up and the price for their product plummeting, found the cost of production exceeding their return on sales. Season after season, they actually lost money.

"Bewilderment, distraction, despair, would come nearer to suggesting the common state of mind as people are forced into selling their most important means of livelihood for less than the cost of production," Caroline Henderson wrote to a friend. "Wheat has been going out of our community by the trainload, 162 carloads in two days from a little siding on our new railroad, at around 25 cents a bushel. It has been as low as 21 cents."

It did not help that momentous changes were taking place in the national diet at the very time demand for wheat was crashing. "Between 1919 and 1928, as families learned that there were vitamins in celery, spinach, and carrots, and became accustomed to serving fresh vegetables the year 'round (along with fresh fruits), the acreage of nineteen commercial truck vegetable crops nearly doubled," said Frederick Lewis Allen. "But the growers of staple crops such as wheat and corn and cotton were in a bad way."

It would not be long before many small farmers were forced out or "tractored out," as many called it. With the new farm machines, it was soon possible to produce a bushel of wheat for each three minutes of labor. In southwestern Kansas, in 1915, there were but 286 tractors. By 1920, the number had risen to 1,333. In 1925, it was 3,051. And by 1930, there were almost 10,000 tractors in just one stretch of the southern plains.

The larger farms soon began to resemble factories in the fields. "My tractor roared day and night, and I was turning eighty acres every twenty-four hours, only stopping for servicing once every six hours," a Kansas farmer wrote, as reported by Douglas Hurt. "A hired man drove the tractor from six o'clock in the morning to six o'clock at night, and the owner drove the remaining twelve hours."

Monster Tractoring— Power to the Farm

The steam engine ushered in the Industrial Revolution in the late-eighteenth century. It remained a fixed-in-place machine until adapted for ships and trains. In the 1870s, the firm of Merritt and Kellogg of Battle Creek, Michigan, began marketing "traction" steam engines that could pull a plow. By the 1890s, such "tractors," as they would eventually be called, could easily plow 45 acres per day.

But as truly monster "local locomotives," what Merritt and Kellogg produced were too big and expensive for the average farmer to own and use. Henry Ford, taking his automobile one step further, so to speak, introduced what he called an "automobile plow" in 1907. Pretty soon, gasoline-powered tractors were "picking up steam," leaving the monster steamers in the "dirt." Yet it was not until 1955 that tractors exceeded the number of horses on American farms.

But with more than a few less-efficient farmers forced to sell their land, where were they to go? Many took to tenancy, working the soil as laborers for the new giant landowners. When tractors drastically reduced the need for their services, rural residents simply fled to the cities by the hundreds of thousands, Between 1920 and 1923, nearly a quarter of U.S. farmers either went broke or bankrupt.

CRASH

To be sure, not everyone was in such desperate straits as the American farmer during the "prosperous" 1920s. Those that were rich, really rich, lived in a world of their own, with more money than they knew what to do with.

In 1929, the top 0.1 percent of Americans had a combined income that was equal to the bottom 42 percent. These super rich controlled 34 percent of all savings. Eighty percent of Americans had no savings at all. In the last year of the decade, Henry Ford reported an income of $14 million; the average personal income was $750.

The moneyed elite had real trouble dispensing their wealth. And that was a problem for the economy as a whole. After all, a family earning $100,000 a year could not be expected to eat 40 times more, and to buy 40 more cars, radios, or houses, than a family taking home $2,500 a year, which was the average middle-class income at the time. The rich could buy only so many goods and services, and their limit on such expenditures was a brake on economic growth.

The more modestly favored, on the other hand, struggled to purchase the products of the new industrial age. In response, they took to buying on credit. By the end of the 1920s, 60 percent of all cars and 80 percent of all radios were bought on the installment plan. Ordinary Americans plunged deeper into debt.

But the rich and poor alike did have one thing in common—both chose to speculate (bet on the future) as if there were no tomorrow, no day of reckoning to come. In the 1920s, they bought stock in American companies as never before.

As long as one believed in the future and was confident that the economy would grow and the price of everything, particularly stocks, would continue upward, there was little to be concerned about. It did not matter what a company was really worth; what counted was what its stock would sell for tomorrow. As long as the amount was more than what was paid today, no problem.

Furthermore, in the 1920s, one could purchase stock on margin: An investor could buy stocks without the money to pay for them. If, for example, a man bought a share of RCA stock with $20 of his own money, he might borrow an additional $80 from a stock broker. If a year later, the stock sold for $400, the investor would have turned his original investment into $316 ($400 minus the $80 and the 5 percent interest owed the broker). That is a return of more than 1,500 percent. No wonder everyone was doing it.

That is, until October 29, 1929, famously known as Black Tuesday, when everything came crashing down. On that day, stocks fell to the point where, at times, there were no buyers at all. Billions of dollars' worth of profits disappeared. Confidence quickly evaporated and with it spending.

The rich stopped purchasing luxury goods and slowed their investing. The middle class and poor stopped buying on credit, fearing their jobs were on shaky ground—which they were. Industrial production fell nine percent between the October crash and the end of the year. As more stores closed, more factories shuttered, and more banks went under, unemployment grew. It was a downward cycle. Soon enough, the Great Depression was a reality.

WE'LL LET YOU KNOW

The "Black Tuesday" stock market crash of October 29, 1929, occurred eight months into Republican Herbert Hoover's presidency. Essentially, the president spent the next four years assuring Americans that though times were not good, they soon would get better. All that was required, his policies reflected, was to let rugged individualism and market forces work their magic.

Given Hoover's conservative, laissez-faire, pro-business assumptions, such a government hands-off approach to what was clearly an economic downturn of unprecedented proportions was not surprising. Yet, in the postwar period, as secretary of commerce in the Harding Administration, Hoover had been credited with supplying American dollars to war-torn Europe, particularly Belgium, in a major relief effort. Why he was unwilling to apply those government interventionist principles at home after the 1929 crash remains a mystery.

Clearly something had to be done. Little more than a year into the new decade, many Americans were going hungry; a few were starving.

"We'll let you know if anything shows up" was the disheartening phrase heard by more than 13 million unemployed as they scrounged, in late 1931, for any kind of work that would keep them and their families alive. Day after day, week after week, the depressing quest dragged on, numbing the ragged searchers. Everything a man owned would have already been sold. He would have borrowed from relatives and friends, most of whom had less and less to give. By 1932, the worst year of the Great Depression, the unemployed were at their wits' end, eagerly seeking relief from the government, however humiliating it might be.

Some men, having lost their jobs, would get up in the morning, dress as usual, and go off to "work." They would stand at the bus or train station, then board and head downtown, all the while putting up a brave front. "In this effort they usually succeeded," wrote Frederick Lewis Allen in *Since Yesterday*. "One would never have guessed, seeing them

Widely blamed for allowing the United States to fall into the depths of the Great Depression, President Herbert Hoover's name became attached to the sad sights that became symbols of the dire era. As people began to lose their homes, shantytowns built from trash became known as "Hoovervilles." Empty pockets were called "Hoover flags," as unemployment skyrocketed to new highs.

chatting with their friends as train-time approached, how close to desperation some of them had come."

"Hoovervilles," or "hobo jungles," sprang up on the outskirts of towns and cities, on vacant lots. Groups of makeshift shacks constructed of packing boxes, scrap iron, and anything that could be picked up free from scrounging junkyards became homes to entire families. The destitute slept in doorways and on park benches by the thousands.

Men and women alike haunted the back alleys of restaurants begging for leftover, half-eaten biscuits. "One vivid, gruesome moment of those dark days we shall never forget," wrote news reporter Louise V. Armstrong in *We Too Are the People*. "We saw a crowd of some fifty men fighting over a barrel of garbage which had been set outside the back door of a restaurant. American citizens fighting for scraps of food like animals."

As bad as things were in the cities, they were even worse in many rural areas. At least during the 1920s, farmers had had a bit of rain. It may not have been economical, given the depressed price of grain, to grow a cash crop, but if pressed to do so, most farmers could plant enough vegetables, potatoes, and the like to feed themselves, a wife, and kids.

In 1930, however, the rains did not come. Planting seeds of any kind made less and less sense. Winds racing through the Great Plains, as always, found the land they whipped exposed. Economic depression, and now drought and windblown topsoil, spread far and wide. The "Dirty Thirties" were at hand.

4. Down and Dusty

"**W**e could see this low cloud bank it looked like," said J.R. Davison, in the film, *Surviving the Dust Bowl.* "You could see it all the way across. And we watched that thing and it got closer. Seemed to kind of grow you know and it was getting closer. The ends of it would seem to sweep around. And you felt like you know you were surrounded. Finally, it would just close in on you. Shut off the light. You couldn't see a thing."

"And it kept getting worse and worse," added Melt White, as part of the film narration. "And the wind kept blowing harder and harder. It kept getting darker and darker. And the old house is just a-vibratin' like it was gonna blow away. And I started trying to see my hand. And I kept bringing my hand up closer and closer and closer and closer. And I finally touched the end of my nose and I still couldn't see my hand. That's how black it was. A lot of people got out of bed, got their children out of bed. Got down praying, thought that was it. They thought that was the end of the world."

It was early 1932, and, along with economic depression, the nation's Great Plains were into the first of what would be seven years of unrelenting drought. The drought was accompanied by gale-force winds that would draw up a 100-million acres of parched, exposed prairie. It had taken a thousand years to deposit only one inch of topsoil, but that topsoil was now being blow away in only minutes.

"When those dust storms blew and you were out in 'em, well you spit out dirt," declared Imogene Glover, a witness, as narrated in *Surviving the Dust Bowl*. "It looked like tobacco juice only it was dirt."

"When I'd see one of these back clouds rolling in," added Margie Daniels, "I remember thinking—why is it so dark? Why is it so dirty? What have I done now? What did we do to cause this?"

On January 21, 1932, the first of many Dust Bowl dusters to come swept across the land, encompassing large sections of five states: the panhandles of Texas and Oklahoma, eastern portions of Colorado and New Mexico, and western Kansas. The dirt cloud, 10,000 feet high, had appeared just outside Amarillo, Texas. Nobody knew what to call it; nobody had ever seen anything like it. "It was like thick coarse animal hair; it was alive," said Timothy Egan in *The Worst Hard Time*. "People close to it described a feeling of being in a blizzard—a black blizzard, they called it—with an edge like steel wool."

In 1932, the weather bureau reported 14 dust storms throughout the Great Plains. In 1933, the number spiked to 38. There would be hundreds more, some lasting days, before the "Dirty Thirties" were done with the greatest environmental disaster in U.S. history.

MISERY IN THE FIELDS

Along with flying, penetrating dirt came a freak of nature that literally sparked the air. Static electricity, the kind that can hurt and injure, tagged on to dusters and swirled, invisible at first, within them. "Mini-lightning," static electricity was not something Great Plains farmers needed on top of their ever-mounting woes.

"I can remember when Dad had a good wheat crop growing and it blew terribly hard for two days," recalled J.R. Davison in *Surviving the Dust Bowl*. "At the end of two days, static electricity, the electricity in the air, had completely killed the wheat crop. All the green wheat had just turned brown and was dead."

The static was so strong in some places that farmers reported watching jackrabbits get electrocuted. They remembered seeing every spike on a barbed-wire fence glowing hot, shimmering electric purple.

As nerve-racking as the electrical storms could be, more serious problems, in both rural and urban areas, spread throughout the land as the Depression deepened. For many, it had reached the point of subsistence, of survival itself.

"American families were reduced to eating dandelions and foraging for blackberries in Arkansas, where the drought was going on two years," reported Egan. "And over the mountains of the Carolinas and West Virginia, a boy told the papers his family members took turns eating, each kid getting a shot at dinner every fourth night."

In May 1932, Caroline Henderson received a letter from a social worker friend in Chicago. She wrote of homes, ". . . where only oatmeal has been eaten for days, where a loaf of bread must serve six children for a meal until relief comes, and of schools where children sit in men's clothing and overshoes. . . . They have gone without food until they do not feel hunger pangs any longer."

Wearing actual clothes to school (as opposed to gunnysacks, which were made of coarse fabric), even if they were a parent's shirt, pants, dress, or jacket, was a "luxury" some households could not match. "In the early years of the Depression, people made clothes from burlap potato sacks, the labels still printed on them, or tore out the seat covers from junked cars and refashioned them into something to wear," Egan noted in *The Worst Hard Time*.

As the drought went on and the winds gained strength, dust storms began to blow through areas of Colorado, Texas, Oklahoma, Kansas, and New Mexico. Referred to by some as "black blizzards," they left houses, farming equipment, and cars buried in what used to be fertile topsoil and covered everything in dust. These storms earned the decade the nickname "the Dirty Thirties."

[I] "made hand towels out of the cement sacks which are no longer returnable; substituted cheap lye for washing powder, so that my hands are rough and uncomfortable from week to week; abandoned regretfully our emergency shelf in the cupboard," explained Caroline Henderson in a letter dated June 10, 1932. "If the President were to drop in for dinner some day,

Hoovervilles

People slept in anything they could find or make. Empty piano crates were a luxury. Most of the destitute were content with putting living quarters together with whatever they could scrounge or even steal: cardboard, scraps of metal, and old mattresses being the favorites. Some even lived in city water mains.

Wherever the homeless and the unemployed congregated (usually in abandoned or undeveloped city lots), the villages they raised became known as *Hoovervilles*, in honor of President Hoover. The term is a spin on the last name of the man many felt had not done enough to relieve their miserable conditions.

The name soon found derivatives. A *Hoover blanket* was the term for old newspapers used as bedcovers. A *Hoover flag* was an empty pocket turned inside out. *Hoover leather* referred to the cardboard used to line worn-out shoes. And a *Hoover wagon* was a horse-drawn carriage, not an automobile.

Even with President Hoover out of office by March 1933, the name Hooverville stuck around, signifying awful living predicaments in both urban and rural areas, until the start of World War II.

he would have to eat wheat porridge or beans or potatoes or cheese or eggs along with the rest of us, unless there was time to prepare a worthless chicken."

That would have been a good meal. For decades, prairie farmers had been feeding tumbleweeds to their cattle. If one ground up "wind witch," as this symbol of the American West was sometimes called, and salted it, the cows would eat it. Three years into the Depression, some farmers were asking if people could do the same thing. The idea was to can thistles in brine. The result was dry as cotton and as flavorless as cardboard, but such "twigs" were supposedly good for you. In 1934, in Cimarron County, out in No Man's Land, officials declared a Russian Thistle Week and urged people who were on relief to get out into the fields and harvest tumbleweeds.

GREAT PLAINS PLAGUES

The droughts brought not only heat, the absence of rain, and windblown soil but also plagues common to the Great Plains that were, in the best of times, troublesome. But now, in these duster-induced worst of times, they were downright unbearable. Cutworms, grasshoppers, and rabbits could literally eat a family out of house and farm.

The cutworm, an inch-long, soft-bodied caterpillar, can consume as much as 75 percent of a crop. The cutworm is a voracious leaf, bud, and, importantly, stem feeder. It got its name because the worm cuts off a seedling at ground level by chewing through the stem. Working mostly at night, the plump, hairy caterpillar attacks and destroys new plants, often dropping several in their burrows. The cutworm ravages more plant than it ever eats.

While cutworms prefer corn, they will attack wheat, alfalfa, oats, and cabbage. Commenting on a generally miserable season in late 1932 (the worst since 1913), Caroline Henderson added cutworms to her grief when she wrote in a letter: "Cutworms in the early spring and a heavy hail storm in May combined to ruin the wheat. The long summer drought brought to nothing all our labor on garden, truck patch and forage crops. We have a dangerously small amount of roughage to see the cattle through the winter and, like everything else, they are worthless to sell. . . ."

If cutworms were bad, grasshoppers were impossible. Natural fungi control grasshopper populations in wet years. During dry times, grasshoppers thrive. And they do so by eating everything in sight. Supposedly, they like salt, and, as a result, will eat the shirt off one's back. They devour anything with a hint of body sweat, including hoe and shovel handles.

Ella Boschma, of South Dakota, reported in *Americans View Their Dust Bowl Experience*: "Grasshoppers consumed everything around the farm. They ate all the garden products, even eating the cork out of the water jug left in the field." When checking a potato patch, she looked down: "The ground was just weaving. And I said 'what is that?' And it was just, they were just hatching by the millions, little tiny things. Folks told stories of cars squishing so many grasshoppers that the roads became slick. There were reports that trains could not make it uphill because grasshopper bodies had greased the tracks.

Then there were the rabbits. A source of food themselves, rabbits also ate food—and lots of it—especially in heavy breeding times brought on by drought conditions. In response, communities organized Sunday rabbit drives on select farms. Local newspapers announced what would often turn out to be a festive occasion, with headlines such as "BIG RABBIT DRIVE SUNDAY—BRING CLUBS."

Timothy Egan describes just such an event that occurred one Sunday at the edge of Dalhart, Texas, as farmers, their wives, and their kids gathered for the kill: "They spread to the edge of the fenced section, forming a perimeter, then moved toward the center, herding rabbits inward to a staked enclosure. As the human noose tightened, rabbits hopped around

In addition to the drought and dust storms, grasshoppers, cutworms, and rabbits began to proliferate throughout the Plains, eating almost everything in sight. In some areas, people counted 10 to 20 insects per square foot, moving about half a mile per day as they continued on to destroy more farms. *Above*, a man in South Dakota looks out a window covered in grasshoppers.

madly, sniffing the air, stumbling over each other. . . . The rabbits panicked, screamed. It took most of the afternoon to crush several thousand rabbits. Their bodies were left in a bloodied heap at the center of the field. Somebody strung up a few hundred of them and took a picture."

HANGING JUDGE

By late 1932, many farmers throughout the Great Plains, particularly in the states of Kansas and Nebraska, had reached the breaking point. On the one hand, growers did not see how they could continue to deliver product to market at below the cost of production. And with debt piling up, farmers were losing their farms; banks were foreclosing, taking back property when an owner fell behind on mortgage payments. On May 3, 1932, in the city of Des Moines, Iowa, despondent farmers gathered to say enough was enough. Thus the Farmers' Holiday Association (FHA) was born.

The association's purpose was to strike—to keep farm products off the market in an attempt to tighten supply and thus raise prices, at least above what it cost to grow and harvest corn, wheat, and other commodities. Association members took to prowling rural roads in an attempt to intercept a "stubborn" farmer's goods on the way to market.

"On a paved road in northwestern Iowa, a truck loaded with cream cans bowls along," began Donald R. Murphy in an article in the *New Republic* of August 31, 1932. "Suddenly a long-chain stretched between two trees bars the road. From the sides of the highway, where they have been lounging under the trees in the tall grass, a dozen tanned men, the leader waving a red flag, bar the road. There are pitchforks handy for puncturing tires, rocks for cracking windshields, and clubs to persuade the truck driver."

Within minutes the farmer's buckets had been dumped all over the road.

The whole strike plan was doomed to ultimate failure, however. As soon as prices rose slightly, farmers rushed to sell their product, and back down went the prices.

Banding together, farmers had better luck stopping the bankers in attempts to foreclose on farms and repossess cattle. With the sheriff standing at his side, a banker would hold a sale of goods and land to a crowd's highest bidder. Farmers got wise to what was happening. Pretty soon they would show up en masse and, having agreed to the plan beforehand, would bid a dime for a cow, a horse, a combine, and so on. Any farmer who attempted to bid higher would be "taken care of" later on. The purchased goods were later returned to the threatened farmer. These 10-cent sales worked for awhile, keeping more than a few last-ditch farmers plowing their land.

In one incident, in Le Mars, Iowa, a judge declined to side with farmers, refusing to swear he would not sign any more mortgage foreclosures. "District Judge Charles C. Bradley was dragged from his court room this afternoon by a crowd of more than 600 farmers," the *New York Times* reported on April 28, 1933. "They slapped him, blindfolded him, and carried him in a truck a mile from the city, where they put a rope around his neck and chocked him until he was nearly unconscious. His face was smeared with grease and his trousers were stolen."

BRING ON THE RAIN MERCHANTS

"Prayer bands have been organized throughout Kansas to end the drought," reported the *New York Times* on July 1, 1934. "The Catholic as well as the Protestant churches in Wichita, Kinsley, Dodge City, Garden City, Liberal, and Hutchinson hold prayer services on behalf of rain."

Three years into the nation's worst drought, folks throughout the Great Plains were now desperate enough to try anything, including prayer, to open the heavens, to drop enough rain to bring in a crop. Five years into the drought, the praying continued. "Because of the dire need for rain in our community and in cooperation with the mayor's proclamation, resting on God's promise 'to heal the land if his people will humble themselves and pray' (II Chronicles, vii, 14), the Christian organizations are sponsoring a day of prayer for rain, Friday, July 10," the *New York Times* reported on July 11, 1936. On June 26, only 0.06 inch of rain fell. A mere mist, 0.02 inch, materialized on July 2.

With prayer less than effective, towns took to bombing the skies in the hopes of releasing water droplets. Tex Thornton, a man with a background as a wildcatter (a person who drills wells in the hope of finding oil in an area not known to have oil fields) and explosives expert, convinced the town of Dalhart, Texas, to pay him $300 in April 1935 to dynamite the air and bring on the showers. He had assured the town that rains in France during the Great War had been caused by continual artillery bombardments. Dalhart was beaten down enough to give it a try.

The plan was to send dynamite aloft with balloons. According to Douglas Hurt in *The Dust Bowl*, "At the appointed hour, several thousand farmers, ranchers, photographers, newsreel cameramen, and reporters gathered to watch the aerial bombing, but a sudden dust storm drove the onlookers to the protection of their cars." Not to be deterred, Thornton next took the opposite tact, burying six charges in the sand before setting the fuse. "The resulting blasts," continued Hurt, "threw additional dirt into the air, where it mingled with the blowing dust, causing even more discomfort to the audience. No rain fell, and Thornton postponed plans for additional detonations."

Desperate measures for desperate times.

5

Black Sunday

In the panhandles of Texas and Oklahoma, Palm Sunday, April 14, 1935, broke clear and serene. On the start of this holiest week of the Christian calendar, townspeople were up, dressed, and off to church, it being clearly a time to give thanks, if not for rain (for there was precious little of that), at least for the absence of a dust storm. There had been 49 dusters in the last three months. Surely, the residents of No Man's Land would be spared the blinding agony of yet another dirt offensive on this sunshiny day.

It was a perfect Sunday for a rabbit drive. One local newspaper called for a "grand and glorious" one "unless the dust is too terrific." As it turned out, the dust this day would be the worst residents of the southern plains had yet experienced—or probably ever would.

About 800 miles north of No Man's Land, near Bismarck, North Dakota, a high-pressure system was battling with a severe cold front that had raced down from the far-off Yukon. As the two weather systems clashed, violent winds churned up massive amounts of dry, pulverized topsoil. In two hours, temperatures plunged 30 degrees. Within no time, the storm

55

crossed South Dakota and entered Nebraska. It was darker and murkier than anything anyone had ever seen.

The duster, a tidal wave of tumbling filth, raced into Kansas and from there straight on to No Man's Land. Rabbits and birds fled in panic. The mother of all Dirty Thirties dust storms was at hand.

"It came quicker than most dusters and was deceptive because no wind was ahead of it," Egan reported. "Not a sound, not a breeze, and then it was on top of them."

What alarmed people was the blackness, as though the Sun had been banished from the sky in an instantaneous cosmic explosion. "It was so dark, you couldn't see the light in the room," one housewife recalled in *Americans View Their Dust Bowl Experience*. "I've never witnessed a darkness so dark."

"The impact is like a shovelful of fine sand flung against the face," wrote Avis D. Carlson in a *New Republic* article. "People caught in their own yards grope for the doorstep. Cars come to a standstill, for no light in the world can penetrate that swirling murk. . . . The nightmare is deepest during the storms. But on the occasional bright day and the usual gray day we cannot shake from it. We live with the dust, eat it, sleep with it, watch it strip us of possessions and the hope of possessions. It is becoming Real. The poetic uplift of spring fades into a phantom of the storied past. The nightmare is becoming life."

The day after Black Sunday, Robert E. Geiger, an Associated Press reporter, wrote a series of articles, the first from Guymon, Oklahoma, for the *Washington Evening Star*. He inadvertently, but appropriately, used the term *Dust Bowl* in describing the region to which he was referring. Almost immediately the public and the press picked up on the expression, using it when referencing the windblown, drought-stricken area centered in the Oklahoma and Texas panhandles—No Man's Land. Thus the term Dust Bowl was born.

JUDGMENT DAY

Margie Daniels, as related in the film *Surviving the Dust Bowl*, remembers Black Sunday six decades after the fact; she still finds it impossible to forget. "When the storm hit, my father just grabbed us," she recalls. "I remember Daddy takin' me and he set us right by the car and he said, 'Stay there! Don't move.' Well, I wasn't about to move. And so then the neighbor man was cryin' and his family was all crying. And so Daddy went over an tried to help 'em and he was stickin' his hankie in the radiator, you know, and puttin' it on his face. And he'd say, 'Oh, God, we're gonna die.' He said, 'We're all gonna die.' And Daddy finally just said, 'Hush. You help me take care of these kids.' That's when he told him he said, 'You take your family in your car and I will bumper you home.'"

When a terrified Kansas farmer tried to drive through the blinding dust of Black Sunday, he got disoriented and drove his car off the road. He was found the next day, suffocated.

Timothy Egan describes the ordeal of Thomas Jefferson Johnson, on a truly fateful day. "Johnson was just a half a block from home when the blizzard overwhelmed him. . . . Felled by the duster, he crawled forward, crossing the road on his belly. . . . The heavy sand blew up his nose and got into his eyes, burning. . . . It felt as if hornets had stung his eyeballs. . . . When Johnson's family found him later in the evening, his eyes were full of black dirt and he said he could not see. He went blind on Black Sunday, and his vision never recovered."

Of that spring in the Dust Bowl, the southern plains, Melt White sums up the misery most felt in describing his mother's reaction to that year of the worst dusters. "In the spring of 1935 the wind blew 27 days and nights without quittin', and I remember that's why my mother just—I thought she was going to go crazy because it was just—it was—you got desperate, because if the wind blew durin' the day or durin' the night and let up, you got some relief. But just day and night, 24 hours,

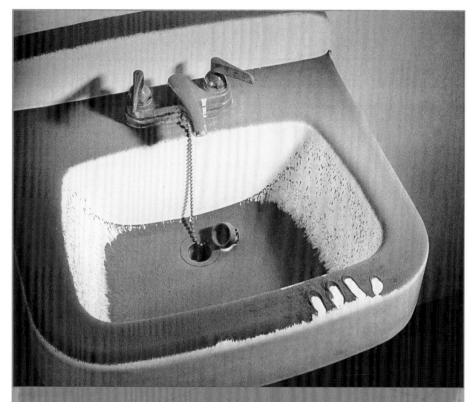

Known as "Black Sunday," the biggest dust storm of the Dirty Thirties struck soundlessly and forcefully, surprising many people as they went to church, enjoyed a Sunday drive, or embarked on a rabbit drive. Dust blackened the sky and blocked out the sun, as surfaces everywhere, like this sink, became covered in dirt.

one 24-hour after the other, it just—but it's 27 days and nights in the spring of 1935, it didn't let up."

For many, the drought and dust storms spreading across their lands were the portent of Judgment Day. "I think the drought was sent to us from God because of the wicked and perverse ways of the people existing today," voiced a Wheeler, Texas, resident. "I go to church more for spiritual guidance and strength. My belief is that God is punishing us for the way we live."

Some felt that farmers just had to accept their adversity without complaint. Writing to a friend in Oklahoma, Texan Evelyn Harris declared, "They forget that the Lord giveth and the Lord taketh away, and that we, as farmers, are powerless to do anything about it either way [when] some other act of God destroys our crops."

Chicago World's Fair

Though its stated purpose was to celebrate Chicago's centennial, the 1933–1934 "A Century of Progress International Exposition" was just as much about vanquishing, as best it could, the Depression from mid-America. It failed in that regard, though the private undertaking did pay for itself. With its motto, "Science Finds, Industry Applies, and Man Conforms," the fair did uplift sprits and gave its approximately 48.8 million visitors reason to hope that once the dark economic times were over, a new day of progress would dawn.

The exposition's exhibits were varied, providing something for everyone. That said, "dream cars" took center stage. There was a Cadillac V-16 limousine. A Lincoln rear-engined concept car was on display. And Pierce-Arrow presented its modernistic Silver Arrow. A Packard won best of show.

And, as part of the fair, promoters in Chicago came up with a novel idea. They went to Major League Baseball and proposed a "Midsummer Classic," a onetime All-Star Game that would pit the best of the National League against the mightiest of the American League. The matchup was such a success, it has been played every year since.

THE GREAT PLOW DOWN

Not everyone believed farmers were powerless, unable to effect change. "Big" Hugh Bennett, the "doctor of dirt" and "father of soil conservation," felt that, with the right approach and correct action, many farm communities in the Dust Bowl could be saved and rejuvenated.

With the election of Democrat Franklin Delano Roosevelt to the White House in 1933, the federal government's approach to dealing with the problems of the Great Depression moved in a dramatic new direction. It was the government's responsibility, the New Deal president believed, to aid those individuals and groups in need—a direct departure from the Hoover administration's laissez-faire, or hands-off, approach. Relief, recovery, and reform, Roosevelt's "three Rs," would thereafter guide federal farm policy.

On May 12, 1933, the president put his signature on the Agricultural Adjustment Act (AAA). Its main purpose was to do something that at first seemed, if not bizarre, contrary to common sense. The AAA would pay farmers not to grow crops or raise animals for slaughter. By either not planting or destroying what had been planted, it was hoped that supply would fall, demand would rise, and farm commodity prices would climb. With more money in their pockets, farmers would start spending, thus raising the economic level of the towns and rural communities that served the farm sector.

Through the AAA, a program was launched in August 1933 to "remove" from market 4 million young pigs and 1 million sows. In the end, more than 6 million light hogs and pigs were destroyed and 222,149 sows slaughtered. Their meat was distributed to various welfare agencies.

The resulting "plow down" (actually, a plow up) of crops or potential crops was "like slitting your wrist" to many farmers, as Egan put it. "In the South, when horses were first directed to the fields to rip out cotton, they balked."

In 1934, the AAA went one step further and actually paid farmers cash to keep land fallow, typically a dollar an acre.

Though, initially, the AAA's efforts did result in a slight rise in farm income, drought and dust storms persisted throughout the Great Plains, land kept blowing away, and most farms remained unproductive.

Hugh Bennett believed that weather was only part of the problem. Man, he felt, was playing a significant and detrimental role. Why was it, Bennett reasoned, that other countries could farm the same type of ground, often for centuries, without losing soil? "Of all the countries in the world, we Americans have been the greatest destroyers of land of any race of people barbaric or civilized," Bennett said, as reported in *The Worst Hard Times*. "What was happening was 'sinister,' a symptom of 'our stupendous ignorance.'"

President Roosevelt summoned Hugh Bennett to the White House. He appointed him head of a new agency, the Soil Erosion Service (SES). Its purpose was to stabilize soil depletion and, if possible, reverse damage already done. With 80-million-plus acres of southern plains topsoil already stripped away, however, and more being blown in the wind every day, Bennett's task was an unenviable one.

THE PLOW THAT BROKE THE PLAINS

Recognizing the need for demonstration projects that would persuade farmers to attempt new soil conservation methods, such as contour plowing and terracing, Bennett set out to put a number of such projects in place. Then, with that behind him, he left, in May 1934, for Washington, D.C., to try and convince lawmakers of the need for an independent soil conservation service.

As Bennett addressed government officials, the skies outside their capital building turned dark, misty, and dirty. Remnants of a huge dust storm, originating 1,800 miles west in the Dakotas, had found their way east to the nation's capital. For Bennett, this was the turning point in gaining necessary public support for all he was trying to accomplish. As the soil conservationist would describe later, "This particular dust storm blotted out the sun over the nation's capital, drove grit between the teeth of New Yorkers, and scattered dust on the decks of ships 200 miles out to sea. I suspect that when people along the seaboard of the eastern United States began to taste fresh soil from the plains 2,000 miles away, many of them realized for the first time that somewhere something had gone wrong with the land." Within a year, Congress had set up the Soil Conservation Service (SCS), the first soil conversation act in the history of the United States or any other nation.

In an expanding effort to publicize the plight of Dust Bowl farmers, the federal government went into the moviemaking business. The result, *The Plow That Broke the Plains*, a haunting, 30-minute black-and-white film, was the first government-sponsored documentary film ever made.

The Plow, produced by acclaimed filmmaker Pare Lorentz (with music written by the equally renowned Virgil Thomson), told the story, in stark terms, of what was going on in the Dust Bowl. It explained what caused the catastrophe and who was in part to blame—the federal government for having, over the decades, encouraged the farming of lands that were never intended to be torn up.

While *The Plow* received widespread critical acclaim and public approval, the film was roundly criticized in the very regions it was meant to expose. Representative Karl E. Mundt, of South Dakota, rose on the House floor to denounce the film as "A drama of distress, from beginning to end." Bad publicity, it would seem, was the last thing politicians wanted for their districts. In 1939, *The Plow* was withdrawn from distribution, not to become available again until 1961.

Like an intense blizzard, large dust storms buried entire farms and houses under a mountain of dirt, trapping people inside their homes. Many houses were covered with 20-foot drifts of sand, leaving only the roofs visible to passersby. Unlike a blizzard, however, people were unable to keep out the dust and dirt, and all available surfaces were coated in grit.

NO LAUGHING MATTER

Not every day in the Dust Bowl was a dirt day. Besides, such days, when they did occur, had advantages, especially for a kid not wanting to go to school. "Snow days" may have kept children home in the East, and, occasionally, during blizzard conditions, in the Midwest, but "dust days" were unique to the Dust Bowl. It was feared that children might simply get lost in a storm and never find their way to or from school. At times, according to Bill Ganzel, "Children were kept in the school-house all night to make sure they wouldn't get lost walking home or be overcome by the dust."

Yet through it all, many found the time and humor to make light of their situation. Jokes about what was happening spread like the wind itself. According to *Wessels Living History Farm*, "People told tales about birds flying backwards during dust storms to keep from getting sand in their eyes."

"Kansas farmers had to pay taxes in Texas because that's where their farms had blown."

"Housewives scoured pots and pans by holding them up to keyholes during dust storms for the sandblasting effect."

"In the middle of the dry years, it got so hot that hens were laying hard boiled eggs."

Yet it was no joke when farmers remembered winds drawing seeds out of the ground, trucks being blown 30 to 40 feet down a street, and chickens going to roost in the middle of the day because a dust storm made it so dark the chickens thought it was night.

And, of course, there was nothing funny at all about a disease unique to the Dust Bowl, dust pneumonia, where, according to *Surviving the Dust Bowl*, "People spat up clods of dirt, sometimes three to four inches long and as big around as a pencil."

Doctors were not sure what it was when they first encountered the seemingly new form of lung infection. But soon enough a pattern of symptoms emerged. According to Egan, "Children, infants, or the elderly with coughing jags and body aches, particularly chest pains, and shortness of breath, began showing up in doctor's offices. Many had nausea and could not hold food down. Within days of diagnosis, some would die." (In 1935, one-third of the deaths in Ford County, Kansas, resulted from pneumonia.)

For many, dust pneumonia signaled that it was time to leave. In 1935, a hundred families in Baca County, Colorado, simply gave their property to the government in exchange for a ticket out of the southern plains. They were sure the land was killing their kids.

On July 26, 1935, Caroline Henderson wrote a letter to Henry A. Wallace, Secretary of Agriculture, in which she declared, "Dust to eat, and dust to breathe and dust to drink. Dust in the beds and in the flour bin, on dishes and walls and windows, in hair and eyes and ears and teeth and throats, to say nothing of the heaped up accumulation on floors and window sills after one of the bad days."

Yet Caroline was not going anywhere; she would not leave No Man's Land. On June 30 of the same year, the 28-year resident of the southern plains had written, "To leave voluntarily—to break all these closely knit ties for the sake of a possibly greater comfort elsewhere—seems like defaulting on our task. We may have to leave. We can't hold out indefinitely without some return from the land, some source of income, however small. But I think I can never go willingly or without pain that as yet seems unendurable."

Most, indeed, were in the Dust Bowl for the long haul. "If only it would rain!" they cried, the land and their lives would be restored.

6 Home on the Plains

By 1936, the rains still had not come. Throughout the Great Plains, from the Dakotas down into Texas, drought persisted, winds blew ceaselessly, and dirt flew everywhere. Drifting topsoil dropped where it was not wanted. Kansas farms wound up in Oklahoma. As wind erosion lifted the topsoil, finer particles such as silt and clay were removed, leaving behind a sandy mixture. The silt and clay, in turn, lifted concentrations of organic matter and plant nutrients. Thus the remaining soil was all the more impoverished and, most critically, left with a lower water-storage capacity.

It is not quite correct, of course, to say that no rain fell during the Dust Bowl years. But it did not rain enough to sustain crop growth. In Nebraska, for example, between 1930 and 1934, rainfall dropped 27.4 percent. As a result, corn crop yields fell more than 75 percent. Farmers, lawmakers, and government officials began to ask, "What kind of agriculture can be practiced in a semi-arid environment?" For some, the answer was simple—none. Better, they figured, to let the land be; let it go back to the native grasses that had sustained it for centuries. Hugh Bennett, himself, had told Congress that 51

66

million acres of the Great Plains had already been so eroded that they could no longer be cultivated. The best that one could hope for was a return, though it would take decades, to preagricultural prairie conditions.

But Bennett also had another idea. Where it made sense to do so, he wanted to set up demonstration projects that would show farmers how to farm wisely and effectively, even in parts of the wind-devastated Dust Bowl. The first such wind erosion demonstration project was begun on 15,195 acres east of Dalhart, Texas. Soon after, similar projects were established in Kansas, Colorado, Oklahoma, New Mexico, and the Texas Panhandle. Each farmer in the region was expected to follow certain recommended soil-use methods and to do so for five years.

One such method was contour plowing, or plowing with the curve of the land, as opposed to straight ahead no matter what the terrain. Although this method is widespread today, it was quite revolutionary for some in the 1930s. If done right, the plowed soil was sure to retain a higher percentage of moisture and thus permit greater vegetative growth.

In 1936, the federal government enabled Dust Bowl farmers to list approximately 4.5 million acres—2.5 million acres of which were contoured. The results were dramatic. According to Douglas Hurt, "A Texas farmer north of Amarillo proved the benefits of contouring when he raised 160 acres of feed on contour plowed land. No one else in his neighborhood had contoured their land and no other feed grew."

The idea, then, as Bennett told President Roosevelt, was to change human behavior, not the weather. "One man cannot stop the soil from blowing," he said, as reported in *The Worst Hard Times*. "But one man can start it." Now, all that was necessary was to get farmers, lots of them, to agree.

RESTORATION AND REMOVAL

Some farmers did agree to try, their situation being that desperate. Previously proud, independent, and entrepreneurial farmers were now begging Washington for aid. "Just show us the way," they told Bennett.

In addition to education and direct funding, farmers needed extra hands to help with all the new work. On March 31, 1933, President Roosevelt had established a federal program that could supply just such aid. Known as the Civilian Conservation Corps (CCC), it would turn out to be one of the most popular and well-received government programs ever put in place.

"First, we are giving opportunity of employment to one-quarter of a million of the unemployed, especially the young men who have dependents, to go into the forestry and flood prevention work," the president announced, after signing the Emergency Conservation Act (setting up the CCC) into law. "We are killing two birds with one stone. We are clearly enhancing the value of our natural resources and second, we are relieving an appreciable amount of actual distress."

Most of the 3 million CCC enrollees who eventually participated in the program were single men, ages 17 to 23. Living in camps, they dug ditches, built reservoirs, planted trees, and helped farmers. They were paid $30 a month, of which they were expected to send $20 home.

At the time of entry, close to 70 percent of CCC enrollees were considered malnourished and poorly clothed. The average worker gained 11.5 pounds in his first three months on the job.

The CCC's slogan was, "We can take it!" With work, marching drills, good food, and decent medical care, most proved they could do the hard physical labor necessary to get land back up to a meaningful level of production.

The CCC established 14 demonstration projects in the Dust Bowl region. "They came from the cities, from universities, from farms in other parts of the country," explained Egan in *The Worst Hard Times*. "In all, about 20,000 workers were sent to the southern plains."

Paradoxically, at the same time the CCC was established, Roosevelt signed an executive order granting federal authorities the power to buy back (retire) lands the government had given away through homesteading over the previous decades. To more than a few, this sounded like a plan to depopulate the plains. Indeed, the Resettlement Administration would give

The Civilian Conservation Corps

The Civilian Conservation Corps (CCC) was a work relief program for unemployed young men. Most participants went to rural camps for six months, where they did heavy construction work. The camps were actually run by the U.S. Army, using 3,000 reserve officers, who became camp directors. By August 1935, there were 502,000 enrollees in 2,600 camps. The average ages were 18–19. Each member earned one dollar per day.

Most participants came from rural areas even though the program hoped to attract city boys. Members stayed in camps, wore uniforms, and lived under quasi-military discipline. They lived in wooden barracks. Enrollees woke up with a bugle call at 6:00 A.M., reported for work at 7:45 A.M., and, after a lunch break, labored until 4:00 P.M. After work, participants were free to engage in sports and take classes. The motto of every CCC worker was "We Can Take It!"

While it did not vanquish the Depression, the original CCC became a model for future state agencies that opened in the 1970s. In 2004, such camps, part of the National Association of Service and Conservation Corps (NASCC), enrolled more than 23,000 young people, primarily in full-time community service, training, and educational activities.

loans to families, allowing them to start anew or buy land elsewhere for the same purpose. With little or nothing left, many farmers signed on to do just that.

"Many of them came by the courthouse," Judge Cowen remembers, in the film *Surviving the Dust Bowl*. "And they'd come by and see me and say, 'Judge, you know, we've reached the end of our rope. We don't have anything left. We've got to get out of here.' And then say to me, 'You know, we need a second-hand tire pretty bad.' Of course, I always signed orders authorizing the local filling stations to get them a cheap second hand tire. Cost about three dollars and a half. And a tank full of gasoline. And they were very pleased about that."

In the end, the Dust Bowl exodus of "Exodusters," as they were called, would turn out to be the largest internal migration in U.S. history.

GETTING ON BOARD

Contour plowing was just one of several methods that could work to stem the stripping of dry land by attacking the twin devils of moisture evaporation and wind erosion.

The lister plow, developed in the late-nineteenth century, plowed, planted, and covered the seed all in one operation. Because of the deep furrows it created, more soil moisture was retained. Furthermore, the lister plow left clods of soil, which meant it was less likely to blow away.

In the 1930s, farmers began using a modified lister, which incorporated a shovel attachment. The shovel built small earthen dams in the furrows every few feet. This "damming" model allowed for twice the moisture retention than on land not so cultivated.

The duckfoot cultivator and the rotary rod weeder also roughened the ground, all the better to prevent soil pulverization. A subsurface packer, equipped with a series of wedge-shaped disks, could break up crusted soil and create deep crevices which caught windblown soil. Various implements

As the Dust Bowl continued, the government implemented agriculture education programs to help farmers maintain their livelihoods but also to prevent further dust storms. Contour plowing *(above)* became one of the more popular methods of farming, as the plowed lines retained more water and prevented topsoil from washing away.

such as these, if used widely and often, could help check Dust Bowl conditions. That is, if farmers would only try them.

Terracing, too, could have a dramatic effect on crop yields, especially when combined with contour plowing. According to Douglas Hurt, "The agricultural experiment station at Spur, Texas, demonstrated by the summer of 1932 that a two-inch rain could be converted into a seven-inch rain when terraces were combined with contour farming. . . . The message was clear—terracing and contouring held moisture in the soil, stimulated plant growth, and decreased wind and water erosion."

Then there was strip cropping, practiced to reduce wind erosion. The method, as described by Hurt, "consisted of planting a close-growing, soil-holding crop such as wheat, alternately with contoured strips of densely growing feed crops such as Sudan, cane, sorghum, or small grains." Grain sorghum could be particularly effective in stabilizing a field because it grew rapidly, to provide a dense, wind-resistant crop.

All these moisture- and soil-retention methods worked, but they had to be applied cooperatively. As Hurt declared, "Although strip cropping alone could not end the wind erosion hazard in the Dust Bowl, when farmers combined it with rough tillage practices and contour farming and terracing, it significantly checked soil blowing."

Still, not all farmers were ready to take such drastic actions, incorporate such "foreign" methods, at least not voluntarily. And since it was vital that all farms in a given region come on board to make the methods work across thousands of acres, the government had to step in with direct incentives, if not downright bribes.

"They came out with a lot of these methods, but most of these old-timers wouldn't do it," reflected J.R. Davison, in the film *Surviving the Dust Bowl*. "You know, finally they got where they'd pay 'em. You know, you could make a dollar an acre if you practiced one of these methods. And that got a lot of 'em workin' on it because they needed that dollar an acre."

SHELTERBELTS

One of the most ambitious Roosevelt New Deal efforts to restrain wind erosion, particularly for future generations of farmers, was the so-called Shelterbelt Project.

With 100 million acres of the Great Plains having lost topsoil, and with half that acreage essentially destroyed (never to be productive again), there were those who wondered out loud whether this vast area, from Canada to northern Texas, was soon to become a desert waste. Given the duration of the unprecedented drought, perhaps hundreds of towns in Kansas, Nebraska, Colorado, New Mexico, Texas, and Oklahoma would simply disappear from the map. Something major had to be done to break the power of wind to gather precious topsoil.

In 1932, as Roosevelt campaigned for president in the bleak, treeless landscape of the northern Great Plains, he hit upon a bold, grand, tree-planting scheme for the region. His "Big Idea" was to plant hundreds of millions of drought-tolerant trees in belts a hundred miles wide, from Canada to Texas. This would create a protected zone, a shelterbelt that would stay the power of prairie winds to destroy the land. As an important by-product, thousands of out-of-work Americans would be employed to make it happen. By mid-July 1934, with funds approved, planting began.

Not all were enthusiastic about the project. Some foresters felt that such a scheme would fail and, as a result, discredit their profession. Others were sure that, at an estimated $75 million over 12 years, the project would be too costly and that money could be better spent on more assured erosion-arresting schemes. More than a few Dust Bowl farmers held back, at first, feeling if success came at all, it would be years, even decades, away. They wanted relief now.

Yet as the project got underway, with hoards of young men from the CCC planting millions of seedlings, attitudes began to change.

A key to acceptance was the tree survival rate. In 1935, it stood at 60 to 70 percent—a good number. As a result, the following year a dramatic increase in planting took place. In Texas, 1.8 million trees were put in the ground. Similar numbers appeared in Kansas and Oklahoma. By July 1, 1936, survival rates ranged from 76 percent in Texas to 80 percent in Oklahoma. The Shelterbelt Project had proven feasible, no question about it.

And as trees sprouted, they grew—fast and tall. In 1938, those planted in Kansas three years earlier were now 18 to 20

As part of another government program, the Shelterbelt Project, young men and farmers planted trees to break the strong winds of the Plains from sweeping through the region and creating large dust storms. The program provided jobs to many unemployed men, including these workers *(above)*, planting trees on an Oklahoma farm in 1935.

feet tall. They were already protecting cropland from wind erosion. In Texas, more than 5 million trees formed 768 shelterbelt miles. And in Kansas, 4 million trees comprised 700 miles of tree belts. Farmer cooperation had turned around, and additional belts, far beyond what was originally envisioned, were brought into the program.

By the end of the decade, when the Shelterbelt Project was terminated, a remarkable level of success had been achieved. True, the trees could not break the wind entirely, far from it. Shelterbelts were limited to reducing wind velocity for a distance of up to 20 times a tree's height (roughly 1,000 feet). And even with 217.4 million trees planted under the project's direction, there were areas not served, and not all trees grew to maturity. Yet when combined with other soil erosion quelling efforts of the 1930s, the Shelterbelt Project had to be seen as worthwhile, having, as Douglas Hurt says, ". . . made a major contribution to the physical and psychological fight against wind erosion and menace."

LAST MAN CLUB

On March 15, 1935, a dust blizzard struck Hays, Kansas. A seven-year-old boy, Khile Salmon, was caught in the storm a quarter mile from home. The next morning, a search party found him covered with dust, smothered to death.

A hundred miles to the west, the same storm stranded the nine-year-old son of Ava Cloud. Found the next day, alive, he was tangled in a barbed wire fence.

Then, on April 30, 1935, the *New York Times* reported that in Springfield, Colorado, "Officials estimated that 'at least twenty' persons have died within the last two weeks in the nation's Dust Bowl of diseases aggravated by the blowing silt." Dust pneumonia was no doubt the cause.

As the Depression and Dust Bowl conditions deepened, some farmers took to "hunting" roadkill. Referring to the desperation felt by many in No Man's Land, Egan declared, "If it wasn't sugar from the bootleggers, which the sheriff gave out free, it was roadkill, which he had his deputies bring in for distribution. There were always takers for critters smashed by a car or a train on a dust-clogged highway or track."

Ironically, when it did rain, it poured, and the deluge did more harm than good. On September 8, 1935, a mother and her four children were found huddled in a cave to escape a storm which blew their farm home away. The accompanying wind then tore the farm house of W.R. Hanna clear off its foundation, sending it rolling over several times before she and her children could escape.

Shelterbelt projects would likely help farmers in the future, down the road a decade or more. But five years into the worst drought the southern plains had ever known, the Oklahoma Panhandle and its surrounding country were blowing dead, turning lifeless. There was no spring planting anymore; no farmers on the road. Maybe it was time to leave. Maybe it was time to move on.

John McGarty, editor of the *Dalhart Texan* and leading citizen of that dust-blown town in No Man's Land, was not going anywhere. John would stay and wait out the storms, and he wanted others to commit to doing the same. On April 15, 1935, he announced the formation of the Last Man Club. Naturally, he was the first to sign up. Others followed, 31 in all. Everyone promised to stay in Dalhart no matter what, never to leave, to be the last man standing. The printed enrollment card read, "Barring acts of God or unforeseen personal tragedy or family illness, I pledge myself to be the Last Man to leave this country, to always be loyal to it, and to do my best to cooperate with other members of the Last Man Club in the year ahead."

Two years later, McGarty left Dalhart for Amarillo, Texas. Nothing personal he told the stunned, slack-jawed town. He had a good job offer in Amarillo and simply could not turn it down. As others across the southern plains prepared to pull up stakes, too, they could only wish that a good job, any job, would be waiting for them in an unknown future.

7 California Dreaming

I t would not be easy, leaving a land one might have homesteaded, a land one had worked a lifetime to bring into fruitful production. Packing up everything, as little as that may have been, and heading west on a mere promise would be life-wrenching. Yet for more than a few, in the Dust Bowl and throughout the Great Plains, the weather had been so cruel for so long that there was nothing to do but try some place new. Drought, Depression, and mechanization—combined they gave one no other choice.

On March 25, 1935, the *New York Times* reported that in Baca County, Kansas, "One hundred families had sought federal aid for moving elsewhere in the last week. A state bank—reputedly solvent, but unable to continue business in the face of the drought—closed at Pritchett."

By the end of the 1930s, 2.5 million people had moved out of the Great Plains states, a quarter-million from the Dust Bowl itself. It would be the largest internal migration in American history.

California, forever seen as a promised land, would be the most popular destination for Great Plains migrants. Handbills that advertised the need for farmworkers in the "golden fields" of California's agricultural "paradise" lured folks west. "300 WORKERS NEEDED FOR PEACHES— PLENTY OF WORK—HIGH WAGES and 500 MEN FOR COTTON—NEEDED NOW!—START WORK RIGHT AWAY!" they declared, as noted in Jerry Stanley's *Children of the Dust Bowl.* In enthusiastic response, Exodusters cried out, "Goin' to Californ-I-A! Goin' to Californ-I-A!"

A mild climate, a long growing season, and a diversity of crops, with staggered planting and harvesting cycles, made California sound unbelievable, almost unimaginable, to a wind-beaten duster. There would be vegetable crops in the Imperial Valley to harvest; oranges to pick in Kern County; and lettuce, cauliflower, artichokes, apples, prunes, and apricots in and around Salinas (near Monterey). The Sacramento Valley would need migrant workers for its asparagus, its walnuts, its peaches, and its prunes. Surely a farmer from the Dust Bowl could, if not start over with his own plot of land, at least find work toiling for others.

They came to be known as Okies (though only 20 percent actually came from Oklahoma), and the migrants grabbed what little they had, abandoned their farms, often not even turning to close the barn door, and headed out, usually onto Highway 66. "They came in decrepit, square-shouldered 1925 Dodges and 1927 La Salles; in battered 1923 Model-T Fords that looked like relics from some antique culture," wrote Frederick Lewis Allen in *Since Yesterday,* referring to those who had successfully made the troubled journey west. "They came in trucks piled high with mattresses and cooking utensils and children, with suitcases, jugs, and sacks strapped to the running boards."

The migrants would leave behind a seemingly depopulated countryside. In 1936, in seven counties of southeastern Colorado, while 2,878 houses were still occupied, 2,811 had been abandoned. Exodusters had simply been driven off their land, tractored out. By 1937, California was receiving an influx averaging one migrant outfit every 10 minutes.

Those lucky enough to have survived the arduous trek, sometimes lasting weeks, or even months, found, however, was that California already had far more agricultural workers than it could possibly absorb. For many, the promise of a new start was shattered in a ruthless competition for little work, at barely livable wages.

THE MOTHER ROAD

But first one had to get there. And while travel by covered wagon was a mode for an earlier time, making the 1,500-mile journey from Texas, or parts farther east, to the California border in the 1930s was often a perilous undertaking. Some would never get to the Golden State, turning back in defeat. A few would die trying.

"The Mother Road—the Road to Flight," author John Steinbeck called Route 66 in his powerful novel *The Grapes of Wrath*, which is about Dust Bowl sharecroppers heading for California. In the book, Steinbeck, a journalist by trade, delivers a number of chapter "asides," where he attempts to remove his "fiction hat" and illuminate conditions as he saw them.

"The dispossessed were drawn west from Kansas, Oklahoma, Texas, New Mexico; from Nevada and Arkansas, families, tribes, dusted out, tractored out," he begins in one chapter, describing destitute and desperate travelers. "Carloads, caravans, homeless and hungry; twenty thousand and fifty thousand and a hundred thousand and two hundred thousand. They streamed over the mountains, hungry and restless—restless as ants, scurrying to find work to do—to lift, to push, to pull, to pick, to cut—anything any burden to bear, for food. The kids are hungry. We got no place to live. Like ants scurrying for work, for food, and most of all for land."

The route itself stretched for 2,400 miles, from Chicago to Los Angeles. If a man picked up the highway in, say, Oklahoma City, he traveled west, through the Texas Panhandle towns of Shamrock and Amarillo. From there, it was direct to

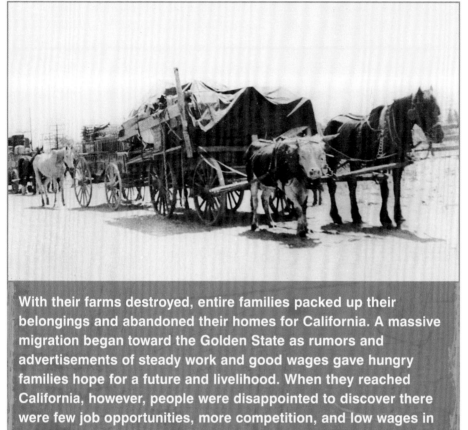

With their farms destroyed, entire families packed up their belongings and abandoned their homes for California. A massive migration began toward the Golden State as rumors and advertisements of steady work and good wages gave hungry families hope for a future and livelihood. When they reached California, however, people were disappointed to discover there were few job opportunities, more competition, and low wages in the farming industry.

Tucumcari and on to Albuquerque, New Mexico, with its blow-torch heat. Next, he would enter Arizona, traveling through Tolbrook, then on to Flagstaff, high in the cold San Francisco Mountains. Onward to Kingman, through the jagged rock of the Black Mountains. Then down into Needles, California.

Yes, California, at last! But this was anything but the lush, green valleys of plenty that migrants had been reaching for. To get there, one had to first traverse the most difficult part of the course, 143 miles of the Mojave Desert, where temperatures in the summer could reach 120°F. "Here there were no towns and few gas stations," Stanley declares. "Here fan belts snapped,

Route 66—
America's Main Street

In *The Grapes of Wrath*, author John Steinbeck wrote, "Route 66 is the path of a people in flight, refugees from dust and shrinking land, from the thunder of tractors and shrinking ownership. . . they come into 66 from the tributary side roads, from the wagon tracks and the rutted country roads. Route 66 is the mother road, the road of flight."

It was also, however, the road of opportunity for those able to see what the flow of migrants might bring. According to Quinta Scott and Croce Kelly, "Despite the dust and the Depression and the flight of their neighbors, there were people who saw an opportunity in what was happening. Those were the people who bought or built highway businesses on the edge of Route 66 and cashed in on what had become a torrent of traffic, catering to the basic needs of food, shelter, and fuel for the people in flight."

From the outset, it was intended that Route 66 would connect the main streets of rural and urban areas to an east-west thoroughfare that would stretch from Chicago to Los Angeles. For those in the Midwest, especially farmers, it provided a road for redistribution of their goods. For truckers heading west, it meant a clear if not straight route through essentially flat prairie lands, in temperate climate.

In 1938, the Chicago-to-Los Angles highway was reported as "continuously paved." Unfortunately, at least for the nostalgically inclined, much of that pavement is, today, cracked and broken. Route 66 is now bypassed with two- and four-lane fast-haul interstate highways.

radiators cracked, and floorboards turned frying-pan hot. . . . One local businessman told the Okies, 'It isn't surprising that you people die along Route 66. The miracle is that any of you make it through at all.'"

Almost always crossing at night, a lone car or a caravan next pushed on to Barstow, at the western tip of the infernal Mojave. From there, on Highway 58, it was straight through the Tehachapi Mountains, and, finally, down into the southern end of California's San Joaquin Valley—a valley that was then, as it is today, one of the most productive agricultural regions on Earth.

DITCHED, STRANDED, AND STALLED

While it is true that some Okies were able to make the trip from the Midwest to California in as little as three days, on as little as $10 worth of gas, and spending most nights in auto courts (the forerunners of modern motels), most had a much harder time of it.

"In July 1935, we loaded some necessary supplies onto a two-wheel trailer and our 1926 model Chevrolet which Jim had overhauled," wrote Flossie Haggard, referring to her husband, as quoted in Michael L. Cooper's *Dust to Eat: Drought and Depression in the 1930s*. "We headed for California on Route 66, as many friends and relatives had already done. We had our groceries with us—home sugar, cured bacon in a lard can, potatoes, canned vegetables, and fruit. We camped at night and I cooked in a Dutch oven. The only place we didn't sleep out was in Albuquerque where we took a cabin and where I can remember bathing."

Ed Holderby remembers his family's trip west, as recorded in *The 1930s: A Cultural History of the United States*. Though Ed did not travel Route 66, instead taking a more northerly path, his journey illustrated the near-starvation conditions he had to endure.

"I recall quite vividly living in a tent at Fort Hall, Idaho, over 4th of July, and eating only potatoes (scrubs and scraps gleaned from behind the digger) for 24 straight days," he said. "On the 24th day, my eldest brother Jim worked from 7 A.M. to noon loading sacks of potatoes into boxcars, with which he purchased a loaf of bread. My mother and my 10-year-old sister, Rosemary, played games like, 'Who can come up with a brand new way to cook potatoes?'"

On the road, few families had money to pay for lodging at night. They just camped on the roadside, often behind or in front of large billboards. Many such billboards depicted the comforts of train travel, showing a man reclining in an easy chair, obviously making the trip out west with ease.

For most Dust Bowl families, however, traveling meant cooking outside, sleeping outside, going to the bathroom in the woods, and bathing in nearby streams. They did whatever they could to make it to tomorrow.

When a car or truck broke down, a common enough occurrence, some of the men in a group hitchhiked to a nearby town in search of temporary work. They might earn 50 cents to a dollar, be able to fix their vehicle, and then head west again.

Dorothea Lange, a photographer who documented the struggles of migrant workers in the 1930s, summed up their plight in a famous photograph entitled "Ditched, Stalled and Stranded." In it, a migrant man sits behind the wheel of his stalled car, staring out in hopelessness, not knowing if he or his family will see another day. Fear and anxiety are clearly visible on his sunken face.

Still, migrants, often traveling in convoys, sought to help each other when anyone faltered. "Us people got to stick together to get by these hard times," a Lange photo caption recalls. It shows a picture of two cars, one stuck in the mud, with occupants of the other standing close by. No one was going anywhere until they all could leave together.

HOBO BRATS

Route 66 was not the only way to California. There were the railroads, particularly the Southern and the Santa Fe. If a Great Plains farmer had a few dollars, he could board his entire family for a pleasant ride west. If he were without money, single, or actually willing to abandon the family, he could still hop the train, but he would have to sneak aboard and ride with the freight. He would become a hobo, a rider of rails.

During the Great Depression, close to 4 million Americans took to the rails in search of work, food, and a place to be. Of that number, a quarter million may have been teenagers and children.

For many, particularly the young, the journey started out as a great adventure.

"We thought it was the magic carpet you know—romance—the click of the rails," said Jim Mitchell in the film *Riding the Rails*.

"I was running into something I thought was an adventure," recounted James San Jule. "For the next couple of years I was a homeless kid riding freight trains."

"One day when school got out—it was the month of June, in 1934, me and another guy caught the first train out," said Guitar Whitey. "There was about twenty guys in the box car and they had to help us up 'cause I couldn't even reach the floor."

Soon enough, however, the thrill of grabbing onto a free ride west turned sour and dangerous. A person could easily fall under train wheels, get trapped between cars, or freeze to death in bad weather. "There was hardly a one who wasn't penniless and half starved much of the time," *Riding the Rails* declared. "Nearly all were looking for work, but in a country laid low—work of any kind was almost impossible to find."

On more than one occasion, a youngster would simply be kicked out of the family, told there was no food for him, and to head west the best he could.

Jimmie Rodgers, later to be dubbed "The Father of Country Music," summed up the loneliness and despair of the hobo life with his song *Waiting for a Train*:

One of the most famous American photographers, Dorothea Lange, captured the hardships of farmers and migrant workers of the Great Depression and the Dust Bowl. Her photographs, like *Ditched, Stalled, and Stranded (above)*, became stark motivators for federal agencies and organizations to create and implement economic and social programs to relieve the suffering of those who had lost everything.

Nobody seems to want me, or lend me a helping hand,
I'm on my way from Frisco, I'm going back to Dixie land;
Though my pocketbook is empty, and my heart is full with pain,
I'm a thousand miles away from home, just waiting for a train.

While many did, indeed, turn around for home (the word hobo may have come from "**ho**meward **bo**und"), most heading out of the Great Plains, bound for California, made it there. What they and their fellow travelers on Route 66 found upon arrival, however, was anything but a welcoming hand.

THE "BUM BLOCKADE"

NO JOBs in California
If YOU are Looking for Work—KEEP Out
6 Men for Every Job
No State Relief Available for Non-Residents

To stop poor people from coming to California, a group of the state's citizens had rented a billboard on Route 66 near Tulsa, Oklahoma. They hoped to dissuade dusters from even attempting the trip west. It did little good.

By 1936, a large number of Californians were tired of the Okies. Migrants, it was felt, were taking jobs away from California natives and swelling state relief roles. In Kern County, on the southern end of the San Joaquin Valley, the health and sanitation budget doubled between 1935 and 1940. The county's education bill, affected by overcrowding, jumped 214 percent. Property taxes rose 50 percent.

Prejudice against the poor, "funny-talking" newcomers expressed itself most cruelly in what became known as Okie jokes. One example: "A tourist and his small son were traveling in California through the cotton belt. The son, upon seeing a cotton picker stand up, asked his father what it was. His father replied, 'That's a cotton picker, son.' The boy after some thought said, 'Daddy, them things look almost like people when they stand on their hind legs, don't they?'"

"When they came over the mountains in 1849, they were called 'pioneers,' now when we come over the same mountains, in 1939, we are called 'migrants,'" an Okie told a reporter in 1936. "Where in the hell did they get that word 'Migrant'?"

Woody Guthrie, a singer and songwriter who documented the Dust Bowl story through dozens of songs written in the 1930s, summed up the paradoxical situation facing these migrants when he wrote the song "Do-Re-Mi," whose refrain contained these lines:

> *California is a garden of Eden,*
> *A paradise to live in or see,*
> *But believe it or not you won't find it so hot, if you ain't got*
> *the do re mi.*

On February 4, 1936, Los Angeles Police Chief James Davis sent 125 of his officers 800 miles to the east, to points along the state line with Arizona. Their purpose was to block and turn back "undesirables." The police were looking for those without jobs or any means of support. Unconstitutional as the action was (Los Angeles police had no jurisdiction outside their city), the "bum blockade," as it came to be identified in the press, had a chilling effect. This was particularly evident when the "border guards" took to practicing their marksmanship in their spare time.

No matter, the migrants kept coming. Such was the lure of the Golden State, in good times and bad. The new "fruit tramps" of the west, migrants who trekked up and down the state looking for any kind of farmwork, were there to make a go of it, come what may.

8 Nightmares in the Promised Land

The San Joaquin Valley, into which road-weary migrants now descended, is part of a much larger 400-mile-long depression running through California, north to south, known as the Central Valley. The San Joaquin, on the south, is the widest section, in some places close to 75 miles wide. It is hot and dry. In southwestern Kern County, less than five inches of rain fall in a year. In the north, there is the Sacramento Valley, drained by the Sacramento River. It is the smaller of the two massive Central Valley subdivisions, but it rains more there, averaging more than 20 inches annually. The Sacramento can sustain itself; crops will grow there naturally. With the San Joaquin, water must be brought in.

When Mexico ceded California to the United States in 1848, vast tracks of land, known as land grants, went with the succession. Thus from the very beginning, to-the-horizon acreage was in the hands of a wealthy few, most of whom owned more land than they could possibly farm, or so it would seem.

Yet as the nineteenth century turned into the twentieth century, Central Valley land barons, particularly in the south, began to visualize the potential beneath their feet, if only water were available. Through theft, shady dealings, and massive purchases over the next few decades, canals and irrigation ditches were built and carved, and water began to flow.

As the Great Depression went on, the U.S. government and charitable organizations organized breadlines and soup lines for the poor. Hungry people, like the man in this famous Dorothea Lange photograph, joined increasingly longer lines in hopes of receiving sustenance.

There was a further requirement to make it all work, however, to get crops from seed to market, and that was an army of low-wage migrant laborers. Given the types of food to be produced (by 1930, there were more than 180 different products growing in California), tens of thousands of hands were needed to plant and gather—and do little else in between. Large-acreage crops, particularly in the south, required infrequent care once they began to rise. Thus while labor would be demanded, it would not be required year-round. Migrants were the answer. These were men who would travel from farm-to-farm, planting and picking, and then disappear in the interim.

Weedpatch

As the Weedpatch Camp, officially known as the Arvin Federal Camp (near Bakersfield, California), struggled to provide temporary shelter to migrant Okies, it became clear that its children would need schooling. But locals wanted no part of "dumb," and in some cases illiterate, Okie kids in their public schools. In response, the courageous Kern County Superintendent of Schools, Leo Hart, took matters into his own hands and created a separate "Okie" school next door to Weedpatch Camp.

The school Hart envisioned would be different. It would be a school that emphasized practical skills—it would be based on industrial arts. In May 1940, Hart declared the school, officially Arvin Federal Emergency School, to be in existence. But as Jerry Stanley pointed out in his book about the school, *Children of the Dust Bowl: The True Story*

At first, such labor was supplied by the Chinese. Seen as a docile, hardworking group of immigrants, they were all that growers could want in a migrant labor force. But then when Californians turned against the Chinese in the late 1890s, the Japanese took their place in the fields. Sure enough, as anti-Japanese feelings exploded a decade later, big-time farmers shifted to *braceros*, Mexican or Mexican-American laborers who handled cotton, fruit, sugar beets, and vegetables with great skill. Finally, growers had exactly what they wanted—or so they thought.

Migrants, of course, would have to eat between planting and harvesting. Thus they would have to be put on relief

of the School at Weedpatch Camp, announcing the school's creation was only the first step: "Weedpatch School started with no grass, no sidewalks, no playground equipment, no toilets, no water, no books, no teachers. . . . It started. . . with two condemned buildings that had been in the field for years and with fifty poorly clad, undernourished, and skeptical youngsters."

To make a go of it, without the use of taxpayer funds, the school would have to rely on donations, literally by the ton, for materials and supplies to construct buildings and sustain operations. In part, to keep Okie kids in their place, that is, out of the public schools, aid from the community did materialize. In the end, the school was built, brick by brick, by the children of the Dust Bowl, eight teachers, and Leo Hart.

In 1944, Weedpatch School was dissolved and absorbed by the Vineland School District. Today, it is known as Sunset School.

during their down time. Up through the 1920s, government payments to Mexican laborers seemed a small burden, the price of doing business, even if it was the citizenry, rather than the farmers, who paid. With the arrival of the Great Depression of the 1930s, however, tolerance for such handouts quickly evaporated. Repatriation took the place of relief. In the 1930s, more than 120,000 Mexicans were given a one-way train ticket to the California-Mexico border. Farmers, who thought they had found an ideal labor supply, now faced a labor shortage.

Down into the San Joaquin Valley came the Exodusters to fill the void. They may not have known how to handle beets, artichokes, oranges, and grapes, but they would learn. Besides, when it came to picking cotton, Okies from the south had no equal. Before long, growers were looking at labor surpluses again—with all the economic advantages such an overabundance of toilers would bring.

WORKING FOR BISCUITS

What happened to the Okies in the latter years of the 1930s, as they swelled the ranks of farm labor throughout California, would speak poorly of how Americans treated the less fortunate among them.

Yes, it was the Great Depression. Yes, at times fully a fourth of those seeking work, any kind of work, could not find it. And true, those fleeing the Dust Bowl could have stayed home as, indeed, most of their neighbors did. But all that aside, there can be little doubt that these new farm laborers, Americans every one, were exploited and abused beyond tolerance. For a few, it would be too much—they would not live to see better times.

The vast majority, of course, survived and passed on their tales of both woe and courage to another generation. At the time, they spoke little of their troubles, being too occupied (and too proud) with trying to make it to another day. Their stories were documented, nonetheless, in the written word, in photographs, and in music and song. Three individuals, John Steinbeck, Dorothea Lange, and Woody Guthrie, emerged to illuminate the plight of migrants in the fields of California.

JOHN STEINBECK

Writing for the *San Francisco News* in October 1936, Steinbeck gave a vivid description of Okies as they entered what all hoped, naively, would be a promised land.

"They arrive in California usually having used up every resource to get here, even to the selling of the poor blankets and utensils and tools on the way to buy gasoline. They arrived bewildered and beaten and usually in a state of semi-starvation, with only one necessity to face immediately, and that is to find work at any wage in order that the family may eat."

In his most famous novel, *The Grapes of Wrath*, published in 1939 (made into a hugely successful movie the following year), Steinbeck depicts in compelling prose just what awaited Dust Bowl migrants and others hoping to flee the poverty of Depression America. Referring to an agricultural contractor, a worker declares, "Maybe he needs two hundred men, so he talks to five hundred, an' they tell other folks, an' when you get to the place, they's a thousan' men. This here fella says, 'I'm payin' twenty cents an hour.' An' maybe half a the men walk off. But they's still five hundred that's so goddamn hungry they'll work for nothin' but biscuits. Well, this here fella's got a contract to pick them peaches or—chop that cotton. You see now? The more fella's he can get, less he's gonna pay. An he'll get a fella with kids if he can."

As Steinbeck was quick to point out, "These new migrants had been small farmers who lost their farms, or farm hands who have lived with family in the old American way." To Steinbeck, Okies were not really cut out for the migrant life. "They are descendants of men who crossed into the middle west, who won their lands by fighting, who cultivated the prairies and stayed with them until they went back to desert," he wrote in the *San Francisco News*. "And because of their tradition and their training, they are not migrants by nature. They are gypsies by force of circumstances."

"Harvest gypsies," Steinbeck called them, charging everywhere in "a gold rush for work."

MIGRANT MOTHER

Dorothea Lange spent years photographing the rich and famous in her San Francisco studio. As the Depression worsened, however, she found it difficult to continue such portraiture. In 1933, as the story goes, she glanced out her studio window to see a breadline of unemployed and homeless men. Lange grabbed her camera and snapped a photo, which she later titled *White Angel Breadline*. She never looked back.

In early 1935, the photographer was hired by the California State Emergency Relief Administration (SERA) to document the growing number of homeless Dust Bowl refugees migrating to California. She wound up taking thousands of photographs (for SERA and other government agencies) throughout the Midwest, along Route 66, and in numerous migrant camps and "Little Oklahomas" in California. Many of her photos are today the iconic images we have of the Dust Bowl and its effects on the land and its people.

In her book *Dorothea Lange: Archive of an Artist*, Karen Tsujimoto describes Lange as "Photographing what she saw—the cross section of migrant laborers ranging from white, Midwest-drought refugees to Mexicans and Filipinos, and the makeshift squatters' camps in which they lived, where shelters were sometimes made of only a few branches, rags, or palm leaves."

Lange reported, "we found filth, squalor, an entire absence of sanitation, and a crowding of human beings into totally inadequate tents or crude structures built of boards, weeds, and anything that was found at hand to give a pitiful semblance of a home at its worst. Words cannot describe some of the conditions we saw."

Born on a reservation in Oklahoma, Florence Thompson became the subject of Dorothea Lange's most famous photograph, *Migrant Mother*. Forced by the Great Depression to become low-wage migrant farm workers, Thompson and her family moved around according to what needed to be harvested.

In March 1936, Lange was returning home after a month on the road when she spotted a sign reading "PEA PICKERS CAMP." There she found a 32-year-old woman, Florence Thompson, with two of her seven children huddled in their makeshift lean-to tent, a battered trunk and empty plate nearby. They had been living on frozen vegetables from the surrounding fields and birds that the children killed. Florence had sold the tires from her car to buy food. The pea crop at Nipomo, California, had frozen, and there was simply no work for anyone.

Lange took six pictures of Florence and her children. One, in particular, later titled *Migrant Mother*, became, arguably, one of the most famous and widely reproduced photographic images of the twentieth century.

It also may have become the most exploited image, if Florence Thompson's later spokespersons can be believed. True, Florence never earned a penny from the photograph. But in reality, as Tsujimoto points out, "Compensation was not the main issue. Rather, the Thompson family remembers that it was embarrassed at being depicted as 'poor,' a condition which, in American life of the time, entailed not only deprivation and hardship but also the burden of generations of social and class stigma. To be poor, no matter how hard one worked, was to be considered somehow inadequate, deficient, shamed."

In the 1930s, being an Okie was synonymous with being poor. It was synonymous with disgrace.

"THIS LAND IS YOUR LAND"

Woody Guthrie, born in Okemah, Oklahoma, on July 14, 1912, wrote dozens of songs and ballads about the poor and downtrodden, particularly his fellow Dust Bowlers. As Guthrie made clear in his autobiography, *Bound for Glory*, he was most definitely one with the people:

"I was thirteen when I went to live with a family of thirteen in a two room house. I was going on fifteen when I got me a job shining shoes, washing spittoons, meeting the night trains in a hotel uptown. I was a little past sixteen when I first hit the highway and took a trip down around the Gulf of Mexico, hoeing figs, watering strawberries, picking mustang grapes, helping carpenters and well drillers, cleaning yards, chopping weeds, and moving garbage cans."

Experiencing Black Sunday firsthand, Guthrie penned the famous line, *"So long it's been good to know yuh."*

Traveling west, as an Exoduster, the itinerate folk singer wrote:

> *We loaded our jalopies*
> *And piled our families in,*
> *We rattled down that highway*
> *To never come back again.*

Upon arrival in California, in the summer of 1938, Guthrie took to wandering around the state singing to migrant laborers. He visited government camps set up to provide a measure of dignity, health, and safety to Okies who qualified to stay in them.

As Guthrie hitchhiked from camp to camp, soon to emerge would be one of his more famous songs, "Dust Bowl Refugees." The first verses summed up the migrants' predicament:

> *Cross the mountains to the sea,*
> *Come the wife and kids and me.*
> *It's a hot old dusty highway,*
> *For a dust bowl refugee.*

In February 1940, Guthrie composed his most famous song, "This Land Is Your Land." In it, the former sign painter, radio host, fruit picker, sailor, dishwasher, and U.S. soldier reached his highest level of class protest. In the final verses, Guthrie cries:

In the squares of the city, In the shadow of a steeple;
By the relief office, I'd seen my people.
As they stood there hungry, I stood there asking,
Is this land made for you and me?

WEEDPATCH CAMP

The Okies were unlike any migrants California had ever seen. In the first place, they were white. Second, they were Americans. More significantly, however, Okies came as a family: a mother, a father, and usually lots of kids. Earlier farmworkers, from China, Japan, and Mexico, were, for the most part, men who had left any family they had back home. Dust Bowl migrants were a package, a family enterprise. They would have survival needs different from those of single men living alone.

As the new, virtually destitute migrants scurried to find work in the fields, they were forced to seek shelter where they could. "These migrants pitched their tents along the irrigation ditches, in empty fields near the large ranches, and in private trailer camps," wrote Walter Stein in *California and the Dust Bowl Migration*. "As the migration reached its peak in 1936 and 1937, the ditch bank settlements grew in size, number, and squalor, and finally became a menace to the Okies themselves and to the resident populations nearby."

Journalists visiting these ditch banks disclosed living conditions that were utterly loathsome. "Hungry Dust Bowl refugees . . . are reportedly living in the fields and woods 'like animals,'" declared the *Berkeley Gazette* in 1937. Actress Helen Gahagan told relief investigators after visiting such a camp, "I went around in a sick daze for hours after witnessing unimaginable suffering."

Steinbeck, in his "The Harvest Gypsies" series written for the *San Francisco News*, talked of a creative sleeping arrangement forced upon a family of six:

In California, communities of migrant camps dotted the landscape in much the same way Hoovervilles had spread across the country. These camps—some of which were government sponsored—housed families who had moved west looking for work.

They have one quilt and a piece of canvas for bedding. The sleeping arrangement is clever. Mother and father lie down together and two children lie between them. Then, heading the other way; the other two children lie, the little ones. If the mother and father sleep with their legs spread wide, there is room for the legs of the children.

In an attempt to deal with the devastation of Dust Bowl migrants, in 1937 President Roosevelt's Farm Security Administration (FSA) built the first of what would be 13 government-sponsored migrant camps near Arvin, a small town 15 miles south of Bakersfield, in the San Joaquin Valley. Known as Weedpatch Camp, it would loom large in Steinbeck's *Grapes of Wrath* as the only respite for his fictional Joad family. In describing Weedpatch Camp to Ma Joad, a small girl whose family had once stayed there, declares:

> Got nice toilets an' bath, an' you kin wash clothes in a tub, an' they's water right handy, good drinkin' water; an' nights the folks plays music an' Sat'dy night they give a dance. Oh, you never seen anything so nice. Got a place for kids to play, an' them toilets with paper. Pull down a little jigger an' the water comes right in the toilet, an' they ain't no cops let to come look in your tent anytime they want, an' the fella runs the camp is so polite, comes a-vistin" an' talks an' ain't high an' mighty. I wish we could go live there again.

With the ability to house no more than 300 families at a time, the self-governing FSA camps could not possibly take in all who pleaded to stay. Besides, the camps provided no source of income for the migrants. For that, they would have to go out into the fields, beg for work at 25 cents an hour, and hope there would be enough food at the end of the day to live until the next. For some, there would not be.

Yet throughout their long ordeal, distressed and dislodged as the Okies were, they remained steadfast and determined. Surely the bad times could not last forever. Someday things just had to get better.

9 Thunder in the Sky

On July 11, 1938, a storm appeared over Amarillo, Texas, just as President Roosevelt's train pulled into the panhandle town of 50,000. Twice that many people were on hand to greet the man they considered their savior.

The storm clouds were dark and rolling, like so many that had appeared in No Man's Land over the past six years of Dust Bowl misery. But as the crowd lifted its collective heads and gazed more intently at what floated above them, it realized that something was different, something was right. This storm was a real storm—one they were sure had materialized to greet their president. It was finally raining water, not land.

"It came in showers at first, the tight clouds frayed at the bottom, and then developed into a downpour," wrote Timothy Egan in *The Worst Hard Time*. "The rain pooled in the streets, and people stood in fast-rising puddles, their shoes wet, to get a glimpse of the President."

What did it mean? Was it just another freak storm, or was this one truly the beginning of the end of the drought that all had been praying for?

"Some cling to the idea that the dust-bowling is over," wrote Caroline Henderson to a friend six months after the president's visit, "but I'd rather wait until March or April or early summer to make a prophecy. . . . We shall wait and see."

On March 28, the following year, Caroline again wrote to her friend. "If you were here tonight you could look out on an Arctic scene instead of the Sahara-like landscape with which you became familiar last spring," she said. "Today has brought low temperature and snow, following a deluge of rain and hail late yesterday. Water flooded in from the road and Mr. H. is gloating [over] the frozen pools of water along his terrace lines."

The Great Plains drought of more than eight years had broken; the Dust Bowl was, at long last, over.

Out west, in California, conditions were changing, too. In 1937, a farmer wrote to President Roosevelt, declaring, "A federal migratory camp is being established adjacent to my property at Porterville, Tulare County, California. . . . Knowing the character of migrants from my experience in dealing with them, I object to these hordes of degenerates being located at my very door." Yet by 1939, initial resentment toward Okies was already mutating into tolerance, if not yet full-fledged acceptance. The Okies were changing, too.

"Under FSA's care, the Okies discarded the physical characteristics that had made them visible on the ditch banks," wrote Walter Stein. "Their accents, of course, remained, but the outward signs of poverty and desperation—the dirt, the skinny children, the ragged overalls—gradually disappeared. Since the Okies were white beneath the grime, the camps made it possible for them literally to scrub off the badge of their inferiority."

With America's entry into World War II, in December 1941, employment to meet the war's needs soared—the Great Depression ended. Okies found jobs in the factories building all manner of war goods. Some, of course, went off to war to do the actual fighting.

Today, migrant camps still exist in California, Weedpatch among them. Currently Hispanics, not Okies, plant and pick the valley's agricultural products. Ironically, the Central

Valley's vast, productive fields are in many cases now owned by Dust Bowl descendants. "First and second generation Okies pretty much run the [San Joaquin] Valley," wrote James J. Parsons in 1987. "The merchants, politicians, and new land barons or growers as often as not trace their family roots back to Texas and Oklahoma."

THE FILTHY FIFTIES

The ending of the Great Plains drought brought a halt to the massive Great Plains dusters, at least the "Dirty Thirties" variety.

The conservation districts Hugh Bennett set up (the only New Deal grassroots operation still in existence) deserve great credit for keeping future dusters weak, in both number and extent. By 1939, 20 million acres in the Dust Bowl region fell into one of the many conservation districts. Getting farmers on board, to manage the land as a single, ecological unit, was having a positive, lasting effect.

In the 1940s, southern plains farmers began to prosper once more. World War II (1941–1945) created a huge demand for wheat, cotton, and beef. New farmers arrived, some of them "suitcase" farmers, to work much of the marginal land abandoned during the Dust Bowl. The rains came, the crops grew, and the black blizzards of the previous decade were often forgotten. Another big plow-up was at hand.

Yet not everyone's memory had turned short-term. "We are kidding ourselves that it won't come again," a western Kansan warned in 1948, as reported by Douglas Hurt. "There isn't a thing being done to prepare for it. If it starts again, within two or three years. . . it will catch us all ill prepared or almost so as it did in the middle thirties. Only this time it will be much more widespread with so much more land broken up out there in Colorado."

By the summer of 1950, drought had returned to southwestern Texas and parts of New Mexico. By 1952, it was again severe in the Dust Bowl region. By 1955, wind erosion had damaged 3.1 million acres in eastern Colorado. Drought and wind were back, and the "Filthy Fifties" had arrived. But not a new Dust Bowl, at least not like anything in the 1930s. Despite the new plow-up, many farmers had learned from their earlier ordeal. As Hurt put it:

"Farmers no longer burnt their wheat stubble. Instead, they used one-way and chisel plows which tilled the soil but left the stubble on the surface. Contour plowing, strip cropping, and grazing management were now standard farming procedures. Furthermore, the Dust Bowl farmers did not have to contend with the financial problems of a depression, and so they were better able to survive the drought and to properly farm their blowing lands."

Though dust did return in the 1950s (plaguing southern plains farmers), many profited from what they had learned in the previous two decades. There was dust, to be sure—but no Dust Bowl.

GLOBAL CHALLENGE

In a scenario that sounds all too familiar, in May 2001, the National Oceanic and Atmospheric Administration in Boulder, Colorado, reported that huge dust storms in western China traveled hundreds of miles east to inundate populous cites, such as Beijing and Shijiazhuang. The storms obscured the Sun, reduced visibility, slowed traffic, and even closed airports. Residents were seen caulking windows with old rags to keep dust particles from penetrating their dwellings. Shades of America's Dust Bowl thirties were at hand.

As with the southern plains Dust Bowl, at first it was thought that China's problem was solely a result of drought. But soon the truth emerged—humans were contributing to the overall destruction. Too many people, too many cattle and sheep, and too many plows, all in an attempt to feed 1.3 billion Chinese, were tearing up the land. China's northwestern provinces were being overplowed and overgrazed, destroying ever

China's growing agricultural industry provides the dirt for dust storms that have reached across the Asian continent, the Pacific Ocean, and all the way to the United States. The soil from these faraway farms at times has covered Beijing in dust, bringing the city to a standstill as airports and roadways are shut down due to low visibility.

more marginal land as wind erosion intensified. People, forced from their communities, were migrating eastward, not unlike the United States migration westward during the 1930s.

Meanwhile, the planet itself is heating up, creating extensive droughts and, with them (where there was also agricultural mismanagement), the possibility of desertification and new dust bowls worldwide. Today's droughts and dust bowls must be seen as part of the greater phenomenon of climate change and global warming, both having become a demonstrated reality. "If droughts and wildfires, floods and crop failures, collapsing climate-sensitive species and the images of drowning polar bears didn't quiet most of the remaining global-warming doubters, the hurricane-driven destruction of New Orleans did," wrote Jeffrey Kluger in the April 9, 2007, issue of *Time* magazine. "Dismissing a scientist's temperature chart is one thing. Dismissing the death of a major American city is something else entirely."

If that sounds a bit over the top, possibly a case of misplaced blame, a report issued by the United Nations' Intergovernmental Panel on Climate Change in February 2007 is even more sobering, if no less certain. "Warming of the climate system is unequivocal," it declared. Furthermore, "There is a very high confidence that human activities since 1750 have played a significant role by overloading the atmosphere with carbon dioxide hence retaining solar heat that would otherwise radiate away."

During the Dust Bowl of the 1930s, there were those who were quick to dismiss what was happening as part of the ever-present dry-wet cycle. Yet, as Don Worster, writing in *Americans View Their Dust Bowl Experience*, summarizes, "There can hardly be any doubt now that the destruction by plow of the grass cover on vulnerable lands—semiarid lands where the soil is loose and the horizon flat and open to winds—has been the leading reason for the devastating scale of dust storms in the twentieth century."

Timothy Egan puts it even more emphatically: "What happened on the hard ground was not a weather disaster at all; it was a human failure."

Consensus as to the human impact on global warming has yet to reach the level of certainty as with the Dust Bowl. Yet blame is moving in the same direction—humans are having an impact, a negative one.

THE HEAT IS ON

In the West, particularly the Southwest, drought is fast becoming the new pattern. "The driest periods of the last century—the Dust Bowl of the 1930s and the droughts of the 1950s—may become the norm in the Southwest United States within decades because of global warming," wrote Alan Zarembo and Bettina Boxall in the *Los Angeles Times*. They went on to point out that, "Computer models, on average, found about a 15% decline in surface moisture—which is calculated by subtracting evaporation from precipitation—from 2021 to 2040, as compared with the average from 1950 to 2000." Tellingly, the authors then state, "A 15% drop led to the conditions that caused the Dust Bowl in the Great Plains and the northern Rockies during the 1930s."

Patrick O'Driscoll, writing in *USA Today*, goes further in spreading the drought and its effects. "Drought, a fixture of much of the West for nearly a decade, now covers more than one-third of the continental USA. And it's spreading." Referring of the summer of 2007, O'Driscoll added, "Half the nation is either abnormally dry or in outright drought from prolonged lack of rain that could lead to water shortages. In central California, ranchers are selling cattle or trucking them out of state as grazing grass dries up."

Lakes Mead and Powell, in the Lower Colorado River Basin, are at half their normal level. Both provide water for more than 30 million people. Neither may ever completely refill.

The threat of another Dust Bowl looms over the future as global warming and climate change have decreased the amounts of available water for personal, professional, and agricultural use. Because nature cannot replenish its resources as quickly as humans consume them, the environmental impact is becoming visible as water levels in reservoirs and lakes dip lower every year, as in Lake Mead *(above)*.

As the climate grows hotter out west, the snowpack that feeds the Colorado River shrinks. More precipitation will fall as rain instead of snow, which is not a good thing. The snowpack will melt earlier, in turn diminishing late spring runoff.

If the drought in the West continues, and the overall supply of water shrinks, how to allocate what is available, between cites and agriculture, will become an urgent issue. Some say it will result in an all out "water war." In such a battle, the urban areas would likely win, and water used to irrigate the fields of California's Central Valley and the like would be diverted. Farms would dry up. Dust Bowl conditions would surface.

If global warming is contributing to increased drought conditions, and global warming is caused, at least in part, by excessive carbon dioxide emissions, then the United States must shoulder a major responsibility for its own predicament.

Buffalo Burgers—Save the Bison

It may seem odd, but by switching from hamburgers to buffalo burgers, Americans could help save the buffalo. Private ranchers, who today raise 97 percent of all buffalo, do so because they can make money selling their meat. As a result, the animals are multiplying. John Cloud, writing in *Time* magazine, puts it this way, "Bison are flourishing again because they have the evolutionary advantage of tasting good and have survived to a time when we all need to eat leaner." He goes on to point out, "We win, and bison win. Of course, the individual bison we eat loses, but the nature of the paradox is that most never would have a chance at life at all if we didn't provide a reason for their husbandry."

Buffalo, it turns out, are leaner than cattle because they range and eat grass. They cannot be fattened the way confined cattle are. Buffalo eat wild grass at essentially little or no cost to ranchers. Unlike cattle, the animals don't have to be expensively fed with corn. Eating buffalo, it can be argued, is good not only for the animal, but for the environment.

Americans ingest the meat of no less than 90,000 cattle per day. That's more than 32 million cattle slaughtered every year to make hamburgers and the like. Maybe it is time to switch, and in the process give both the buffalo and the cattle a break?

North Americans send 15.7 metric tons of carbon dioxide per capita into the air every year. That compares with 2.6 metric tons for Asia and 2.3 metric tons for Latin America. In the United States, 33 percent of emissions are from vehicles, 28 percent from industry, 21 percent from homes, and 17 percent from businesses. Clearly, the heat is on.

"THE PRAIRIE ACRE"

The southern plains never fully recovered from the Dust Bowl dirt blizzards of the 1930s. The Dust Bowl era ended conclusively in 1941 when the region received more rain, 33.25 inches, than it had at any other time in the twentieth century. And the drenching continued throughout the decade.

Still, those living and farming the vast, flat plains remained forever wary, never quite sure that the bad times were banished for good. Caroline Henderson, for one, "Had faced too many blizzards and hot summers, too many crops ruined by drought or flood, too many dust storms, to look optimistically again at her world of No Man's Land," said her editor, Alvin O. Turner. "She now dreaded each new year, anticipating fresh disasters, which all too often arrived on time." Caroline died, at the age of 89, on August 4, 1966.

Today, the plains, as in the past, cannot rely solely on rain to grow crops year after year—there simply is not enough moisture falling from the sky. Instead, farmers must turn downward, deep beneath their land, for water salvation. The mighty Ogallala Aquifer, the nation's biggest source of underground freshwater, lying beneath the Great Plains from South Dakota to Texas, is now (thanks to advanced technology) being pumped to the surface at a rate of 1.1 million acre-feet a day. A day! As Timothy Egan points out, "That is a million acres, filled to a depth of one foot with water." The aquifer is being drawn down eight times faster than nature can fill it.

But all has not been dissipated. In parts of the Great Plains, there is a return to what used to be—in a way. "Thousands of

Native Americans long off the 'rez'—Blackfeet, Crow, Flathead, Northern Cheyenne, Sioux—are putting the white man's cities behind them and heading for home," reported John G. Mitchell, for *National Geographic*, in May 2004. "A lot of these people returning from the cities are retirees. This is where they want to be. This is where their heart is."

And the buffalo are back. Not, of course, in the numbers of old, but in surprising numbers nonetheless. It seems a taste for their meat, leaner than that of beef, is spurring ranchers to raise the bison on private land and in private herds. In March 2007, *Time* magazine reported that there were now roughly 450,000 bison roaming North America. And there is talk of expanding National Bison Ranges, where the mammoth creatures can roam free and wild as in the Old West.

Today, on the campus of the University of Kansas, a spot of land is set aside. It is exactly one acre. Students are free to roam this "Prairie Acre," as it is designated, to read, to relax, and to take in the grass, the trees, and various other prairie flora. Set aside by the university, it is there to show all who come what it was like before settlers took to tearing up the land, working it, and making it their own. It is there to remind people that there are times when it is best to leave Mother Nature alone.

Chronology

1929   October 29. Stock market crashes, ushering in the Great Depression.

1931   Drought hits the Great Plains and lasts eight years.

1932   Black blizzard dust storms begin throughout the Great Plains.

1934   **May 9:** A dust storm travels from the Dakotas to the Atlantic, dropping 300 million tons of soil.

1935   **April 14:** Black Sunday, the most devastating Dust Bowl storm of the 1930s.

1936   March. Dorothea Lange takes "Migrant Mother" photograph.

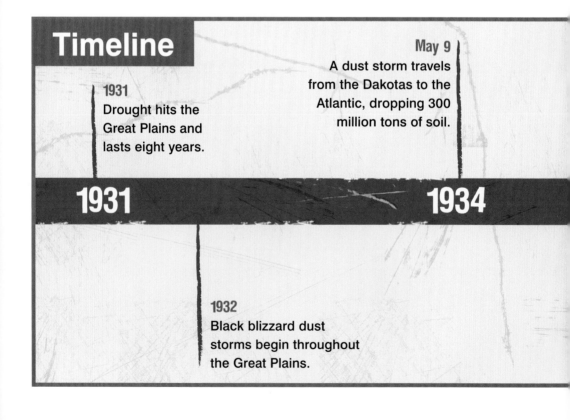

Timeline

1931
Drought hits the Great Plains and lasts eight years.

May 9
A dust storm travels from the Dakotas to the Atlantic, dropping 300 million tons of soil.

1931

1934

1932
Black blizzard dust storms begin throughout the Great Plains.

1937 **April 15:** Last Man's Club organized in Dalhart, Texas.

May 10: Premier of the documentary *The Plow That Broke the Plains*.

Farm Security Administration opens up first migrant camp, "Weedpatch," in Arvin, California.

1939 John Steinback's *Grapes of Wrath* is published.

Rain begins to fall in the Great Plains, ending the eight-year drought and the Dust Bowl.

1940 The movie *The Grapes of Wrath* premiers.

1941 The United States enters World War II.

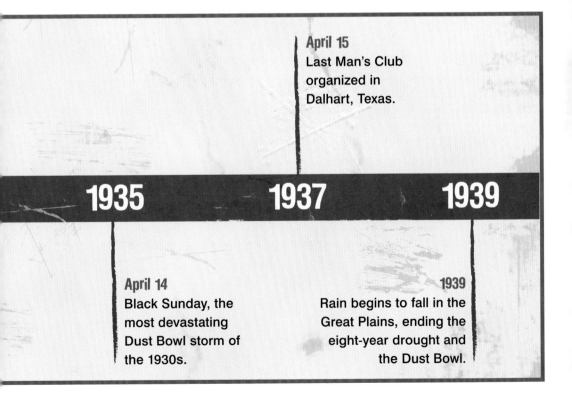

April 15
Last Man's Club
organized in
Dalhart, Texas.

1935 — 1937 1939

April 14
Black Sunday, the
most devastating
Dust Bowl storm of
the 1930s.

1939
Rain begins to fall in the
Great Plains, ending the
eight-year drought and
the Dust Bowl.

Glossary

aquifer   A water-bearing stratum of permeable rock, sand, or gravel. An underground lake.

Armageddon   A decisive conflict, confrontation, or catastrophe.

barbed wire   Twisted wires armed with barbs or sharp points; used for fencing.

buffalo   Also know as bison; an animal with short horns, heavy forequarters, and a large muscular hump that was abundant on the Great Plains until practically exterminated in the late-nineteenth century; now raised commercially.

Chinook   A warm, dry wind that descends the eastern slopes of the Rocky Mountains.

Dust Bowl   A region that suffers from prolonged droughts and dust storms. The catastrophe of the 1930s.

duster   A dust storm.

erosion   The process of wind and/or water eating away or slowly destroying the land.

flapper   Young women of the 1920s who showed a great deal of freedom from social conventions.

foreclosure   A process whereby a bank or lending agency takes over a property when the holder can no longer make mortgage payments.

global warming   An increase in the Earth's temperature widely believed to occur because of to an increase in greenhouse gases because of pollution.

harvest   To gather in a crop, to reap it.

hobo   A homeless person, usually a penniless vagabond. Also a migrant worker.

insolvent   Without money.

land grant   A large grant of land made by the government, usually for agricultural or educational purposes.

laissez-faire   A doctrine opposing governmental interference in economic affairs. Literally "let alone."

list   To plant in ridges with a lister.

migrant worker   A person who moves regularly in order to find work, especially in harvesting crops.

moldboard   A curved iron or wooden plate attached above a plowshare to lift and turn the soil.

New Deal   The legislative and administrative program of President Franklin Delano Roosevelt that was designed to promote economic recovery and social reform.

Okie   A migrant agricultural worker from the Dust Bowl region.

plow   A farm implement for cutting, lifting, and turning over topsoil.

prairie   A large area of level or rolling land in the Mississippi and Ohio river valleys that—in its natural, uncultivated state—usually had deep fertile soil; a cover of tall, coarse grasses; and few trees.

reaper   A machine for harvesting grain.

Serengeti   A large grassland in Africa that, in the nineteenth century, was filled with lions, antelope, elephants, cheetahs, giraffes, zebras, hyenas, and dozens more species.

sod   A short grass, turf, covering the ground.

sodbuster A farmer who came to the Midwest to farm by breaking up the tough sod.

suitcase farmer An absentee farmer who owns or leases the land but does not work it.

thresher A farm machine designed to separate seed from a harvested plant.

topsoil A surface soil, usually including the fertile organic layer in which plants have most of their roots and which the farmer turns over in plowing.

wildcatter One who drills wells in the hope of finding oil in territory not known to be an oil field.

Bibliography

BOOKS

Allen, Frederick Lewis. *Only Yesterday*. New York: Harper & Row, 1931.

———. *Since Yesterday*. New York: Harper & Row, 1939.

Durden, Mark. *Dorothea Lange*. New York: Phaidon Press, 2006.

Egan, Timothy. *The Worst Hard Time*. New York: Houghton Mifflin, 2006.

Ganzel, Bill. *Dust Bowl Descent*. Lincoln: University of Nebraska Press, 1984.

Henderson, Caroline. *Letters from the Dust Bowl*. Norman: University of Oklahoma Press, 2001.

Hunt, Douglas R. *The Dust Bowl: An Agricultural and Social History*. Chicago: Nelson-Hall, 1981.

La Chapelle, Peter. *Proud to Be an Okie: Cultural Politics, Country Music, and Migration to Southern California*. Berkeley: University of California Press, 2007.

Lott, Dale F. *American Bison: A Natural History*. Berkeley: University of California Press, 2002.

McKnight, Tom L., and Darrel Hess. *Physical Geography: A Landscape Appreciated*. Upper Saddle River, N.J.: Pearson Prentice Hall, 2008.

Nash, Gary, and Julie Roy Jeffrey. *The American People: Creating a Nation and a Society, Volume II*. New York: Pearson, 2006.

Partridge, Elizabeth. *This Land Was Made for You and Me: The Life and Songs of Woody Guthrie*. New York: Viking, 2002.

Starr, Kevin. *California: A History*. New York: The Modern Library, 2005.

Stein, Walter J. *California and the Dust Bowl Migration*. Westport, Conn.: Greenwood Press, 1973.

Steinbeck, John. *The Grapes of Wrath*. New York: Penguin Group, 1939.

Tsujimoto, Karen. *Dorothea Lange: Archive of an Artist*. Oakland: Oakland Museum of California, 1995.

Watkins, T.H. *The Hungry Years: A Narrative History of the Great Depression in America*. New York: Henry Holt, 1999.

Wunder, John R., Frances W. Kaye, and Vernon Carstensen, eds. *Americans View Their Dust Bowl Experience*. Boulder: University Press of Colorado, 2001.

NEWSPAPERS

"Huge Dust Cloud, Blown 1,500 Miles, Dims City 5 Hours." *New York Times*, May 11, 1934.

"Heat in Midwest Increases Drought." *New York Times*, June 2, 1934.

"Dust Storm Kills Four in Midwest." *New York Times*, March 17, 1935.

"Colorado Families Flee Dust Storms." *New York Times*, March 25, 1935.

"Dust Victims Pray for Oklahoma Rain." *New York Times*, April 15, 1935.

"Dust Deaths at 20: New Storm Rolls." *New York Times*, May 1, 1935.

"Shelterbelts Pressed." *New York Times*, June 23, 1935.

"Family in Cave Refuge." *New York Times*, September 9, 1935.

Steinbeck, John. "The Harvest Gypsies." *San Francisco News*, October 5, 1936.

"Drought Migration Left Many Ruined." *New York Times*, March 1937.

Boxall, Bettina. "Warming Expected to Intensify Basin Drought." *Los Angeles Times*, February 22, 2007.

Boxall, Bettina, and Alan Zarembo. "A Permanent Drought Seen for Southwest." *Los Angeles Times*, April 6, 2007.

O'Driscoll, Patrick. "A Drought for the Ages Spreads Across U.S." *USA Today*, June 8, 2007.

MAGAZINES

Brown, Lester R. "Another One Bites the Dust." *Earth Policy Institute*, 22 February 2007.

Cloud, John. "Why the Buffalo Roam." *Time*, 26 March 2007.

"Flee Dust Bowl for California." *Business Week*, July 3, 1937.

Fanslow, Robin A. "The Migrant Experience." *American Folklife Center*, April 6, 1998.

Mitchell, John G. "Change of Heartland: The Great Plains." *National Geographic Magazine*, May 2004.

Kluger, Jeffrey. "What Now?" *Time*, 9 April 2007.

FILM

The Great American Experience, *Surviving the Dust Bowl*. 1998.

The MARPAT Foundation, *The Plow That Broke the Plains*. 2005.

WEB SITES

A Geographer Looks at the San Joaquin Valley.
http://geography.berkeley.edu

Farming in the 1930s.
http://www.livinghistoryfarm.org

Route 66 Highway.
http://www.route-66.com

The Handbook of Texas Online.
http://www.tsha.utexas.edu

Weedpatch Camp.
http://www.weedpatchcamp.com

Further Reading

Cooper, Michael L. *Dust to Eat: Drought and Depression in the 1930s*. New York: Clarion Books, 2004.

Heinrichs, Ann. *The Dust Bowl*. Minneapolis: Compass Point Books, 2005.

Janke, Katelan. *Survival in the Storm: The Dust Bowl Diary of Grace Edwards*. New York: Scholastic, 2002.

Nishi, Dennis. *Life During the Great Depression*. San Diego: Lucent Books, 1998.

Press, Petra. *A Cultural History of the United States*. San Diego: Lucent Books, 1999.

Stanley, Jerry. *Children of the Dust Bowl: The True Story of the School at Weedpatch Camp*. New York: Crown Publishers, 1992.

Turner, Ann Warren. *Dust for Dinner*. New York: HarperCollins, 1995.

Picture Credits

Index

About the Author

RONALD A. REIS is the author of 15 books, including young adult biographies of Eugenie Clark, Jonas Salk, Lou Gehrig, Ted Williams, and Mickey Mantle.